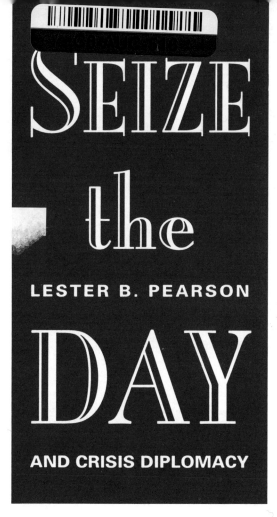

SEIZE the

LESTER B. PEARSON

DAY

AND CRISIS DIPLOMACY

GEOFFREY A.H. PEARSON

Seize the Day

LESTER B. PEARSON AND CRISIS DIPLOMACY

by

GEOFFREY A.H. PEARSON

CARLETON UNIVERSITY PRESS
Ottawa, Ontario
1993

© CARLETON UNIVERSITY PRESS, INC. 1993
Printed and bound in Canada

CANADIAN CATALOGUING IN PUBLICATION DATA
Pearson, Geoffrey, 1927-
   Seize the day : Lester B. Pearson and crisis diplomacy
   Includes bibliographical references and index.

ISBN 0-88629-216-6 (bound) -
ISBN 0-88629-217-4 (pbk.)

1. Pearson, Lester B., 1897-1972. 2. Canada – Foreign relations. 3. Canada –
Politics and government – 1935-1957. 4. Canada – History – 1945-1963. 5. Prime
ministers – Canada – Biography.
I. Title.

FC621.P4P43 1993   971.064'3'092   C93-090497-4
F1034.3.P4P43 1993

Carleton University Press
160 Paterson Hall
1125 Colonel By Drive
Ottawa, ON Canada
K1S 5B6
(613) 788-3740

Distributed in Canada by:
Oxford University Press Canada
70 Wynford Drive
Don Mills, ON Canada M3C 1J9
(416) 441-2941

Cover and interior design by CARRIE COLTON DESIGN.

Acknowledgements
   Carleton University Press gratefully acknowledges the support extended to its
publishing programme by the Canada Council and the Ontario Arts Council.
   The Press would also like to thank the Department of Communications,
Government of Canada, and the Government of Ontario through the Ministry of
Culture, Tourism and Recreation, for their assistance.

To

The Members of The Canadian Foreign Service,

Past, Present and Future

ACKNOWLEDGEMENTS

WITHOUT ACCESS TO the files of the Department of External Affairs I could not have written a diplomatic study of this kind. John Hilliker and the staff of the historical section of the department helped me to locate these and to search for missing documents. Don Barry of the University of Calgary was in the midst of writing the second volume of the departmental history and saved me from many a wrong turn. The staff of the National Archives of Canada, and especially Maureen Hoogenraad who for many years has been a devoted guardian of my father's papers, introduced me with good humour to the mysteries of archival research, and Marjorie Bull and her staff at the library of the department were always ready to provide a congenial atmosphere in which to work. Former colleagues in External Affairs, including John Hadwen, Douglas LePan, Lois Macintosh, Mary MacDonald, Geoffrey Murray, Escott Reid, Basil Robinson, Arnold Smith and Paul Tremblay, either read parts of the manuscript and gave me useful comments or helped me to recall the atmosphere of the times. Christopher Young and Greg Donaghy took the trouble to read the whole text and to offer suggestions. Jackie Shaw helped me with chapter 4.

Robin Hannah typed succeeding drafts for little reward and Diane Mew, my editor, polished the final product with her customary authority. If rough edges remain, I kept them there. Finally, I am grateful for the encouragement and advice of Michael Gnarowski, Jennifer Strickland and Anne Winship at Carleton University Press who never appeared to doubt that this enterprise was worth doing despite the worries of its progenitor.

TABLE OF CONTENTS

PREFACE

THE RISKS OF filial piety for a writer have been pointed out so often that it hardly seems necessary to repeat them here. Having decided to run them, however, I owe the reader some explanation. There is at least one great advantage for the son or daughter who writes about a parent — a special point of view based upon a particular kind of experience and knowledge to which no-one else can lay claim. In my own case, this point of view has been sharpened by having spent most of my career in the profession of diplomacy, a profession that L.B. Pearson abandoned only with reluctance and that set its stamp upon his approach to public life. Moreover, he was unable to complete the volume of his memoirs dealing with his time as the Secretary of State for External Affairs from 1948 to 1957, and no-one else has examined this period both from the inside and from his own perspective.[1]

I was not myself close to all the events described hereafter, having been at Toronto and Oxford universities from 1948 to 1952 and at the Canadian embassy in Paris from 1953 to 1957. But I was in frequent touch with my father and was aware of how he regarded the principal issues of policy. I have chosen to examine these issues as a series of challenges or turning points, some of them ending with decisions to proceed along new paths of policy, others remaining unresolved. They are distinct events and yet illustrative of a time and an approach to policy that both reflected and strengthened a Canadian vision of the future of international relations. We might say now that Canada was "on a roll." True, it was a period defined by the special circumstances in which Canada found itself after the war. Circumstances create opportunities, they do not ensure results. Pearson and his colleagues sought to take advantage of them for the benefit, as they believed, of both Canada and the world.

GEOFFREY PEARSON
July 1993

INTRODUCTION

THIS IS A BOOK about Canadian diplomacy from 1948 to 1957 when Lester B. Pearson was the Secretary of State for External Affairs. If you look up the word "diplomacy" in Roget's Thesaurus you will be directed to expressions dealing with "cunning," "mediation," and "compact." As for the first, diplomacy has long been associated with trickery and sharp practice, especially since Machiavelli gave advice of this kind to princes in the sixteenth century. Diplomats represent governments and carry out instructions; if these are based on deception, then the diplomat deceives. Or the diplomat may misinterpret or distort his instructions. In either case, diplomacy has failed. The task of the diplomat is to state the policy of his or her government as precisely as that policy allows. Of course, the same virtues of honesty and precision apply to other professions.

Not many professions are concerned with mediation, however, if by that is meant the settlement of disputes by peaceful means; and no other profession deals primarily with disputes between sovereign states. The notion of "compact" comes closer to the classic definition of diplomacy: the management of international relations by negotiation and, in a more limited sense, the application of tact and discretion to such management. But, as we shall see, there are other aspects to diplomacy, including in particular the public expression of policies and goals, which go well beyond negotiations as such. "History in action," Pearson called it somewhat incautiously in an early attempt to describe Canadian diplomacy.[1]

As a minister of the crown, Pearson was also responsible for formulating policy, and the factors which helped to determine foreign policy will also be considered in the following pages. While the diplomatic function is to execute policy and not to make it, a neat separation of the two is rarely possible. This was especially so in the postwar Department of External Affairs, where senior officers were not only "present at the creation" of much of the postwar structure of international security and commerce, but actively helped to build it. As one of those who was there has noted, "diplomats are thus not just the executants of the designs of others. They participate in the creative task of making the designs."[2] Pearson had himself been a diplomat for twenty years. He saw no great change in function as he switched from one office to another in the East Block of the Parliament Buildings, and he treated his colleagues in the department in more or less the same way as before. But as Secretary of State, he had less uniform and more critical constituencies to nurture — the cabinet, the House of Commons, and the public.

The trade of diplomacy, sometimes called the second oldest profession in the world,[*] was simpler forty-five years ago than it is today. There were far fewer independent states (about sixty) and therefore fewer diplomats. There was little or no television and most diplomats did their work anonymously and in secret. Heads of state and of government did not travel as much, leaving the bulk of the work to their ambassadors on the spot. The latter were largely concerned with political and trade issues; they were less involved than they are now in the details of immigration policy, for example, or the tribulations of tourists. Nevertheless, the image of the diplomat as negotiator of secret treaties was already beginning to look a bit faded. The United Nations and other international agencies created after the war were as much public as private bodies, and diplomats were having to learn to play to the gallery and to brief the press. Conferences of all kinds multiplied. As new states joined Embassy Row, the social round of national day receptions and other public occasions took up more time. Pearson fitted easily into this more public world, never himself having been entirely comfortable in the more rarefied atmosphere of the backroom.

The nature of the department over which he was to preside for nine years will be discussed in chapter 1, and the main questions of policy which faced that department in 1948 will be noted in chapter 2. The

---

* John Holmes said he was prepared to argue, however, "that Eve's negotiations with the snake in the Garden of Eden entitle diplomacy to be called the oldest profession." Unpublished manuscript, "A Career in the Foreign Service," undated.

following seven chapters will deal with some of the principal policy decisions that he had to make as minister during the period. A final chapter considers the basic ideas or themes that gave these decisions coherence in what has been described as the "Pearsonian consensus." This is not therefore a history, much less a biography, in the usual sense of those terms. It is a study of diplomatic method in a particular period and of the various factors that help to explain both its high reputation at the time* and its continuing relevance.

First, however, it may be useful to consider the subject matter in a more general way. What can we learn from a study of Canadian diplomacy of this period? One historian has remarked of the Victorian period in England that "the greater part of what passes for diplomatic history is little more than the record of what one clerk said to another clerk."[3] If we take "clerk" to mean "official," high or low, then that judgment may be true of most diplomatic history before 1945. The revolution in communications technology and a new emphasis on human rights have changed the context of diplomacy in more recent years. Public opinion is now often cited by governments to justify the policy of the moment. American public opinion, for example, was a crucial restraint on Canadian diplomatic initiative after 1945, not only because US officials so frequently invoked its authority, but because of the influence it exerted on Canadian opinion. The rhetoric and ideology of the Cold War, as we shall see, provoked a kindred freeze in public attitudes, making dissent or even criticism unpatriotic, if not downright treasonable. Canadian diplomacy was faced with a double challenge: how to convince Washington to act as a partner rather than an overlord in its relations with Canada and others; and how to persuade our European allies and Commonwealth friends that Canada itself was a partner and not a satellite of the United States. It met the challenge, by and large, through a combination of diplomatic networking, military cooperation, and independent initiative that kept Canada-US relations for most of the time on a basis of respect and confidence and enhanced Canadian influence elsewhere.

---

* A reputation, it may be noted, that appears to be all but unknown to American historians of the period. Perhaps this is because as James Eayrs puts it, "it is the Canadian style to try to garden in the field of politics, not to dam or dredge." (*The Art of the Possible*, [Toronto: UTP, 1961], p. 154).

This was not a view that all Canadians shared. Pearson was sensitive, for example, to criticism from the CCF (now the NDP) that Canadian policy was too beholden to the strategic vision of Washington, whether in its assessment of the Soviet threat, its judgment of Chinese intentions, or the militarization of NATO at the expense of its political and economic functions. Canada, it was said, was more "powder monkey" than "peace-maker."[4] But this was a minority view, even amongst students of foreign policy. Neither the universities nor the press had produced more than a handful of such students, and members of Parliament paid little attention to the subject except in times of crisis. Not until the 1960s did the minority view gain prominence, in part because the prospect of detente with the Soviet Union was helping to dissolve the Cold War attitudes of a generation before.

The idea of peace-maker was closely allied to the goal of independence in foreign policy. Later, Prime Minister Pierre Trudeau confused the critics by emphasizing the second and not the first. He set out to fashion a more "realistic" approach to the conduct of policy by appearing to give priority to such factors as the quality of life and the safeguarding of sovereignty, an approach that was meant to separate Canada's interests in North America more sharply from those of the United States. In the end, however, he was deeply involved in the role of 'peace-maker'; nor did it prove possible to reverse the gradual integration of the Canadian and United States' economies. Perhaps the idea of "liberal internationalism" is not, after all, incompatible with the concept of closer economic relations between the two North American neighbours.[5]

Lester B. Pearson, for one, had no reason to believe during these years that expanding trade with the United States would hamper Canada's freedom of action on the world stage. The government of Louis St. Laurent, on the contrary, was preoccupied by the reluctance of the United States to engage in freer trade and to foster cross-border development, for example, by the construction of the St. Lawrence Seaway. Good neighbourly relations, Pearson believed, were a condition of maximizing Canadian influence in Washington on the main issues of international policy, such as east-west relations and the management of regional conflict. And so it proved during the international crises of the period. Canadian independence was not, in his mind, to be measured in dollars but in values, and he never tired of warning Americans against the dangers of excessive patriotism and militant anti-communism. He believed above all that one legacy of the war — international cooperation to stop aggression through the United Nations — had somehow to be preserved during the years of Cold War antagonism, and that the invention of nuclear weapons made this task ever more urgent. It is to these twin themes of an active Canadian diplomacy and a vision of world order that the conclusions of this study are devoted.

CHAPTER ONE

The Minister and the Department in 1948: From King to St. Laurent

WHEN LESTER B. Pearson was appointed as Secretary of State for External Affairs on 10 September 1948 at the age of fifty-one, he had been in Ottawa for two years as the Under-Secretary of the department. His minister for that period had been Louis St. Laurent, for whom he had developed a strong and abiding affection.[1] St. Laurent was 13 years older than Pearson and from a quite different background. They were not friends, therefore, in the usual sense of that term, and I don't recall ever seeing St. Laurent in our home. But of course they had worked together closely and they shared much the same views on foreign policy, views that sometimes alarmed the Prime Minister, Mackenzie King.[2]

Pearson was closer to two other ministers, Brooke Claxton, Minister of National Defence, and Paul Martin, Minister of National Health and Welfare, both of whom had been appointed to these positions shortly after his return to Ottawa from Washington, where he had served as Ambassador in 1945–46. Both had a deep interest in foreign affairs and had kept in touch with Pearson before and during the war. His service in London and Washington had also kept him in touch with some of the Members of Parliament on both sides of the House of Commons, including Gordon Graydon and James Macdonnell, friends from University of Toronto days. But by the same token he had had little opportunity to become familiar with the House and its inmates.

The East Block of the Parliament buildings, where the Prime Minister had his office and the Department of External Affairs was housed, was a different matter. Jack Pickersgill, assistant to the Prime Minister, and Arnold Heeney, Clerk of the Privy Council, were both good friends and knew all there was to know about the Ottawa agenda.

Unlike his predecessor as Under-Secretary, Norman Robertson, Pearson had not been a member of the elite group of wartime public servants headed by the long-time Deputy Minister of Finance, Clifford Clark, who planned and implemented Canada's postwar economic policies.[3] But his participation in the founding of the United Nations agencies dealing with food and agriculture (FAO) and with refugees (UNRRA), as well as the fact that Canada was a member of the UN Economic and Social Council from 1946 to 1948, helped to ensure that Robertson's transfer from Ottawa to London as High Commissioner to the United Kingdom would not seriously weaken the Department's capacity to shape policy on the new international economic order.

Pearson would not have wished to serve in a Mackenzie King cabinet. King's inhibitions about accepting new international commitments and instinctive "Canada First" policies were foreign to him. King had spoken to him about entering politics as early as August 1946, and had returned to the subject a year later.[4] But it was not until King announced his retirement in January 1948 and Louis St. Laurent became the heavy favourite to succeed him at the party convention in August, that the possibility of a political career began to be taken seriously. St. Laurent was elected leader of the party on 7 August (defeating Jimmy Gardiner, the veteran party politician from Saskatchewan with whom Pearson had little in common) and spoke to Pearson shortly afterwards about joining the cabinet.[5] Pearson was ambivalent about this prospect. On 1 June he had written to Norman Robertson in London about the Ottawa scene, noting that if a minister from the cabinet were to be chosen to succeed St. Laurent "it will, I think, be Brooke Claxton, but there are other ideas in which I am directly involved." He added: "However, in this regard at least, I am master of my own destiny, and feel that I should think, and think two or three times again, before abandoning bureaucracy for politics." He did, indeed, think hard about this invitation, as I well recall. He was concerned about what he would do if the party or he himself were to be defeated in the election of 1949, only a year away. But after Mr. St. Laurent put the question in terms of "service to the country" there was never much doubt about his response. My mother was less than enthusiastic about a political career but old friends reassured him. Hume Wrong, who followed him at the Washington post, wrote: "I am sure you would be a success as a politician."[6] The future beckoned.

The New Minister

Lester Pearson entered office at a propitious time. The new Prime Minister was popular in the country and the undisputed leader of his party. He was greatly respected by his Ministers and presided over the cabinet with authority and dispatch. His relations with Pearson remained excellent, and indeed have been described by Paul Martin as "unique in Canadian affairs."[7] Their rapport extended to questions of domestic policy as well. In November 1950, for example, my father wrote to me that he was a member of the "ginger or left wing group" in the cabinet on matters of social policy, and that this group had the support of St. Laurent. As a junior Minister, Pearson no doubt had to give a respectful hearing to the views on foreign policy of more senior Ministers, especially those of C.D. Howe, the Minister of Trade and Commerce, who was in charge of Liberal party fortunes in Ontario and who had helped Pearson win his seat in the constituency of Algoma East (where he was to be re-elected seven times). Moreover, he was aware that veteran politicians do not always look kindly on civil servants who join their profession without going through the years of apprenticeship on the back benches that is the usual lot of Canadian politicians. But neither Howe nor others were prepared to question the main lines of foreign policy, or challenge the St. Laurent-Pearson team, even if they harboured doubts about the new activism, which on the whole they did not unless substantial new expenditures were involved.[*] Conversely, Pearson was the first to admit his ignorance of

---

[*] Foreign policy was a regular subject of cabinet discussion, however. In addition to Pearson, St. Laurent and Brooke Claxton (who acted in Pearson's absence) were the main participants. In the months after Pearson joined the cabinet its agenda included items on the situation in Europe, North Atlantic security, Palestine, the change of regime in China, and Commonwealth affairs. Then and later the cabinet frequently had to decide on the export of arms to areas of tension. See NAC, RG2 A5A, reels T2366 and T2367, Cabinet Conclusions.

subjects to which Howe and Douglas Abbott, the Minister of Finance, gave priority, such as fiscal and industrial policy: "I'm afraid I don't know what to do, or indeed much about the problem [of inflation]," he informed me in February 1951. The new Minister had two great advantages: he was a professional who knew his subject better than his colleagues, and he presented his views with tact and charm. By 1948 both style and views had been fully formed.

"The style is the man himself," it is said. But style has also been called "the dress of thoughts." Both aphorisms have been applied to Pearson. He was blessed with an equable temperament and physical stamina. These attributes, combined with an upbringing as the son of a Methodist minister, which encouraged both self-confidence and sobriety, were identified in later years with an easy informality (the bow tie), frank speaking (the background press conference), and a cheerful disregard for status and hierarchy (an indifference that nevertheless later appealed to Queen Elizabeth, who awarded him the Order of Merit in 1970).

His mind was broad rather than deep; good enough to qualify him for a job teaching history but not such as to persuade him or others that scholarship was his métier. His interests were bound up with his work, but he found time for reading (mostly history and current affairs) and he enjoyed music and the theatre. As a small boy I was introduced to most sports, his favourite method of relaxation. He wrote well and often, rarely accepting the material prepared for him without refining it into his own distinctive mixture of anecdote and paradox. He combined a quick wit with a fund of stories and was popular at Ottawa dinner parties. Unlike most of his diplomatic colleagues, he enjoyed talking to the press, on and off the record. In 1938–39 he had even been tempted to join the fledgling CBC.

He was not an orator in the parliamentary sense and partisan declamation was foreign to him. But his wit and informality, as well as the command of his material, were powerful aids to the job of selling his policies to Canadian and American audiences, a job that he performed with energy and enthusiasm. It was this record of public speaking that led to the widespread expectation by the early 1950s that he would run for the leadership of the Liberal party, although the motive for his public activities was that of the salesman who has more faith in the product than in the company.

His upbringing led him to value things of the spirit, but these were rather the biblical parables of the "good" life than the mysteries of the Cross or the ceremonies of the church. He drew strength from the vicissitudes of life; a favourite hymn was "Say not the struggle naught availeth," and despite the experience of two world wars he retained a basic optimism about human nature. I rarely, if ever, found him depressed or self-pitying, although he could be easily upset by mischance or stupidity. He had the self-confidence of those who play well, whether or not they win, appearing to have learned from some guardian angel "to treat those two impostors, Triumph and Disaster, just the same." Indeed, he had grown up with Kipling and had imbibed the aura of the playing fields of Eton.

His contemporaries recognized in him some of the chief qualities of diplomacy — patience, tolerance, flexibility, a sense of proportion, and moral imagination. But they also noted a distaste for confrontation, an emotional distance, which my sister and I came to know as children and to exploit at times. Able to see both sides of any dispute, he would turn it aside with a joke or a story.* He reached always for the middle ground. Perhaps this is why some observers claimed to perceive a complex man who rarely revealed his real intentions and carried within him a secret self. George Ignatieff, a close adviser, has commented: "I never knew whether my advice was being rejected or accepted."[8] I doubt myself that any mystery lurked behind the facade of reticence. He witnessed at an early age the brutality and squalor of the First World War and, like others, may have suffered some darkness of the soul, to be repressed or overcome by a quick wit and a sense of paradox. He was, above all, a man of action, impatient of delay, obfuscation, or double-dealing. The springs of this activity are to be found in a set of moral attitudes and beliefs, which were pervasive, if not always logical or clearly articulated.[9]

These beliefs went beyond those of the family of a Methodist minister, schooled in the homilies of the Protestant faith and the

* He once said that the chief distinction of a diplomat was that "he could say no in such a way that it sounded like yes," Department of External Affairs, S/S 47/1.

simple pleasures of the baseball diamond. His uncle, the Reverend R.P
Bowles, Chancellor of Victoria College, was proud to justify in print
his belief in pacifism, and his father, the Reverend E.A. Pearson, would
deliver sermons in the same vein ("as patriots, we must get rid of war,"
he told a congregation in Toronto in 1927). Pearson's own experience
of war in the Balkans continued to haunt him in 1934, when he
described "its horror and unutterable degradation" to a church group
in Ottawa.[10] He put his faith in the League of Nations, and when the
League failed, in the creation of a new international organization with
the capacity to deter or resist aggression. The United Nations was
regarded by its founders, including Pearson, as an instrument for the
application of "collective security," by which they meant a concert of
the powers to prevent war, if necessary by the use of force. Canadian
officials argued at first that force ought to be used against great and
small powers alike if they committed aggression, but in the end they
had to accept that such a threat, if carried out, could precipitate a
world war. They came to hope, however, that to threaten such use
against lesser powers would effectively prevent war, or at least serve to
prevent a greater war. The abhorrence of war that Pearson felt
convinced him to accept the consequences of enforcement action if
they helped to prevent a third descent into Armageddon.[11]

He also believed, however, that if the great powers were unable to
work together to prevent war a balance of power was the safest way to
keep the peace. The use of the veto by the Soviet Union in the early
years of the UN led directly to the creation of a North Atlantic security
organization, NATO, in 1949, which Pearson and St. Laurent defended
as the best means of preventing war in the absence of a wider system
of security. Pearson tried to cloak NATO in an economic and social, as
well as military garb, and if he had to accept finally that such clothes
did not fit, he continued to hold to the universalist ideas he had
sought to implement after the war. They were restated in his memoirs
twenty-five years later.

A third belief, held strongly throughout his career, was distrust of
national sovereignty as a basis for international cooperation, and of the
national interest as a guide for foreign policy decisions if this were to
be interpreted in a narrow or short-sighted way. Modern science and

communications, he often said, made interdependence inevitable and peace indivisible. The answer was to be found "in a voluntary surrender of some measure of sovereignty to a world authority in the interest of peace and security."[12] He rarely quoted Mackenzie King, but he agreed with King that "above all is humanity." As late as 1970 he repeated this idea: "human sovereignty transcends national sovereignty."[13] Such ideas, it may be argued, are not always a useful guide to action; obviously, the indivisibility of peace implies the indivisibility of war. But in general, these precepts, pointing as they do towards cooperation rather than competition in the affairs of humanity, were the source of that spirit of practical idealism that eventually led to the Nobel Prize.

Finally, and despite this international stance, Pearson was a strong nationalist, staking out positions for Canada in the postwar world that amounted to a drastic break with past policies. Canada's record in the war was the basis for these positions. But the inspiration for establishing them came from the two diplomats who, in Geneva, London, and Washington, had suffered most from the prewar caution and egoism of Mackenzie King: Hume Wrong and Pearson himself. Both had watched the failure of the League from front-row seats and both had deplored the reluctance of Ottawa to face up to the European crisis. They had chafed under British and American tutelage during the war and took the lead (Pearson in Washington, Wrong in Ottawa) at the end of the war in ensuring for Canada an appropriate place in the hierarchy of postwar international institutions (the origin of what came to be known as Canada's "middle power" status). They shared with King a strong suspicion of tendencies in London to re-forge the links of empire, but they rejected King's instinct to isolate Canada from such tendencies, favouring instead a more activist Canadian foreign policy. Pearson was more publicly outspoken than Wrong about shaping the peace, and perhaps less realistic about the prospects, but both were determined that Canada take part in the process. "What was new," John Holmes has recalled, "was the more active and positive will in Canadian foreign policy."[14] And Pearson reflected in his memoirs: "To me, nationalism and internationalism were two sides of the same coin."[15]

The Chief Lieutenants

Arriving in office with these views, Pearson was fortunate, not only in the backing of his Prime Minister, but in having about him a group of men who were his friends as well as his advisers. Those who combined the two functions most nearly were Norman Robertson, Hume Wrong, Escott Reid, and Arnold Heeney. Arthur Schlesinger, the American historian who worked in the Kennedy White House, has described five kinds of advisers: pragmatic, analytical, ideological, manipulative, and sycophantic. He noted that most advisers play several or all of these roles.[16] Pearson's main advisers were above all pragmatic and analytical, with Reid adding a dose of ideology.

Born in 1894, Wrong was the oldest of the four and the first to join the fledgling foreign service in 1926. Pearson, a colleague of Wrong's in the Department of History at the University of Toronto, joined a year later, and Robertson, ten years younger than Wrong, in 1929. Reid and Heeney did not arrive in Ottawa until some ten years later, and their relations with Pearson were less close. Still others, such as Hugh Keenleyside, H.F. Feaver, Tommy Stone, George Glazebrook, Alfred Rive and later, Charles Ritchie, Jules Léger, George Ignatieff, Saul Rae, Gerry Riddell, Arnold Smith and Charles Hébert, were to become good friends but were not then in senior positions in Ottawa.

Inevitably, there had been a certain rivalry among Wrong, Pearson, and Robertson, "The Three Musketeers" of Canadian diplomacy which, coupled with differences in personality, has led some to speak of tensions that allegedly interfered with their relations after 1948.[17] Robertson was an intellectual whose catholic interests ranged from wheat futures to nineteenth century French literature. His favourite recreations were walking his dog, bridge, and conversation. Wrong was less of an encyclopedia and more of a dictionary. He was a draftsman rather than a talker, who cared about precision, order, and meaning, and wielded a legendary blue pencil. "You may 'think'," he said, "but not 'feel'." Both men were sons of professors and had taught at universities themselves. Robertson preferred to work by exchanging views; Wrong preferred to analyse and to plan. I recall, as a child, that Hume Wrong, with his blind eye and severe countenance, seemed a more distant figure than NAR (as he was known), who laughed readily and seemed to take a kindly interest in you. In later years I came to know Robertson better than Wrong (who died in 1954) and to share his interests in literature and ideas. They were both greatly admired by their juniors. A factor often overlooked in the relations of the three men was the friendship among the wives, and indeed among the three families. They spent holidays together in the Gatineau hills near Ottawa (where they are buried side by side), they had common friends outside the Department, and the Wrongs and Pearsons were in London together in the early years of the war.

The early success of Robertson (he became Under-Secretary at the age of thirty-seven) and the later move of Pearson into politics probably tended to magnify what differences of temperament there were between them, but I know of no evidence that these impaired their working relations. Wrong was in Washington as Ambassador from 1946 to 1953, after which he served as Under-Secretary until his premature death at the age of fifty-nine. Robertson served as Clerk of the Privy Council from 1949 to 1952 and then returned to London as High Commissioner, a post at which he thrived and where he achieved an outstanding reputation (the London *Times* described him on his death in 1968 as "a diplomatist of world rank"). Wrong established an equally high reputation in Washington. He became a close friend of Dean Acheson, the Secretary of State during the Truman administration, and was an incisive analyst of the American scene at a time of uneasy relations with Canada. Both men were indispensable collaborators of Pearson, as their correspondence with him amply demonstrates (not many ambassadors today would address their Minister by his nickname) and as his tributes to them on their deaths testify.[*]

Escott Reid, who describes himself in his memoirs as a "radical mandarin," joined External Affairs in 1938, served for three years in Washington, and then spent more than ten years in Ottawa, the last three as the Deputy Under-Secretary under Arnold Heeney.[18] From

---

* Pearson wrote of his friendship with Robertson that "it was strong enough to adapt itself easily and without constraint to the changed conditions brought about by my desertion of the External Affairs service for politics." It is signficant that he should still speak in 1968 of his leaving the public service as "desertion" ("External Affairs," September 1968).

1947 to 1952 he worked closely with Pearson, at once gadfly, philosopher, and "holy obstinant."[19] His memoirs are remarkable for their generosity towards his colleagues, and for their unsparing attention to his own sins of omission and commission. His zeal, allied with a creative imagination, at once attracted and exasperated his seniors, especially Hume Wrong, with whom he crossed swords over policy towards the United States. Pearson liked to test new ideas against the conventional wisdom of diplomacy, and Reid provided them. He was one of the architects of the postwar system. His later service in India as High Commissioner left an equally impressive mark on Canada's relations with that country. In the words of one who has studied his career, he was "the mandarin who seemed to see farthest ahead."[20]

Arnold Heeney, like Robertson and Reid, was a Rhodes scholar, and like Reid and Pearson, the son of a clergyman. He had served as Secretary to the cabinet for nine years when he was appointed to fill Pearson's shoes as Under-Secretary in January 1949, a post he served in until going to NATO in 1952. He was ambitious (but who wasn't at that time in Ottawa?) and made no secret of his desire to secure the Washington embassy as soon as possible, an objective he achieved in 1953. Heeney had established his reputation as an administrator, no doubt the main reason that Pearson recommended his name to St. Laurent as the new Under-Secretary (he was the first deputy from outside the foreign service and would be the only one until 1983). In addition, however, Pearson knew him well and liked him. He had an easy, direct, and confident manner, both at work and at play (his relations with Pearson were assisted by the fact that he played tennis). He was not, as Reid was, a student of international politics, but with Pearson as his Minister he did not need to be. His job was to manage the department, then experiencing some strain as its activities multiplied faster than its resources. He commented to Robertson in London soon after taking over that "the atmosphere in the Department and the confidence among the senior officers are not what they should be," perhaps reflecting the fact that there had been a five-month hiatus at the top.[21] Manage the department he did, to the general satisfaction of his Minister, who was thus liberated to pursue the goals of policy he had long sought.

The East Block
In 1948 the Department of External Affairs was still relatively small compared to other departments, but expanding fast. The staff had almost doubled in the past two years, reaching a size of some thirteen hundred persons serving at Ottawa and at twenty-nine posts abroad. Most of these were in Europe and the Americas, including two new offices accredited to the UN in New York and Geneva. Posts sent to Ottawa about 45,000 letters and telegrams in 1948, and many of the telegrams received had to be deciphered by hand. The capacity of the one hundred or so officers in Ottawa to deal with all this material was strained to the limit, especially as many of them at any one time were called upon to attend the ninety international conferences in which Canada participated that year.[22] However, staff quality was high, and their numbers included many who had served in the armed forces during the war and who were anxious to continue to serve Canadian interests in this new and almost equally adventurous role. University professors, such as R.A. Mackay and R.G. Riddell, recruited originally for emergency service, stayed on. Competitive examinations were reinstituted in 1947 and attracted some fifteen to twenty-five new officers annually thereafter, 90 per cent of them male (women were required to resign if they married and there was no female head of post until 1953).

A weakness in the Canadian government of the time was the relative lack of incentive for French-speaking Canadians to join. External Affairs was no exception. Business at headquarters was conducted almost entirely in English, a handicap for young officers from Quebec who had little choice but to learn to write in English if they wished their advice to be taken into account. Veterans of the department from Quebec, such as Jean Désy and Pierre Dupuy, preferred to work abroad, and Laurent Beaudry, the Associate Under-Secretary, who had remained in Ottawa during the 1930s and 1940s (partly to act as friend and counsellor to new recruits from Quebec), retired in April 1948.[*] Nor were English-speaking

---

[*] Beaudry is one of the unsung heroes of the department, partly because he worked in such low-profile areas as consular and legal affairs. Robertson described him "as a man of great charm and integrity of character, and a most loyal and unassuming colleague" (Pearson Papers, vol. 1, 10 February 1947) St. Laurent offered the post of Under-Secretary to Jean Désy in November 1948, no doubt in order to compensate for Beaudry's retirement, but was turned down (NAC, St. Laurent Papers, MG26 L, vol.89, Pearson to St. Laurent, 25 November 1948).

officers required to learn French until some years later, a fact which
Pearson and Robertson always regretted not having done something
about earlier (neither spoke French with any proficiency). A determined
attempt to improve matters was made by Marcel Cadieux when he
became the head of the Personnel Division in 1949. He published that
year a book on the department in French, addressed principally to
university graduates in Quebec. In it he set out to demystify the practice
of diplomacy and to awaken the patriotism of young Quebeckers.
Cadieux, who was later to become Under-Secretary, thought of the
foreign service as a kind of calling, not unlike that of a monastic order.
He warned his potential recruits that they would have to display "une
attitude spéciale qui ressemble à celle du soldat. Le soldat obéit." And he
appealed to their idealism: "un idéal de vie austère certes, mais digne et
profondément respectable."[23] Cadieux had only limited success, not
surprising given the climate of the times. When I joined the foreign
service in 1952 five of the twenty-five entrants were Francophones, but
only three came from Quebec.

Cadieux's ideal foreign service was far from the popular image of
diplomats as social butterflies, flitting from one salon to another. Was it
accurate? He had served as executive assistant to both Robertson and
Pearson and knew what was expected of the monks in their cells on the
third floor of the East Block. Pearson's choices for senior level
appointments to the department in January 1949 did indeed reflect an
aptitude for dedication, if not exactly for contemplation. Reid remained
as the number two official, to incite the rest to think globally and in the
King's English. Gerry Riddell, who had become one of the first
exponents of the "middle power" thesis at the UN, was asked to help
Pearson write the speeches that would lay out the principles of an active
foreign policy (his death in 1951 of a heart attack was a great blow to
Pearson). John Holmes, also a former teacher and war recruit, who had
served in London and Moscow, took Riddell's place as head of the UN
division. George Glazebrook, another Toronto professor, was persuaded
to head the Joint Intelligence Board and thus to strengthen the position
of External in that area, and Wynne Plumptre, an economist and a
former student under John Maynard Keynes who was respected by the
high priests in Finance, took over the Economic Division.

Men like these were not dilettantes. But neither were they monks. Most had families and they enjoyed what they could of the sparse fare of Ottawa cultural life, as well as seeing a great deal of each other socially. Work perforce came first, however, and it is probably fair to say that they felt most at home when in the office. The songs of Saul Rae, head of the Information Division, offered a welcome diversion, but these too were usually about life in the East Block. Charles Ritchie, who returned to Ottawa from Paris in early 1950, has described the situation of the Dedicated Civil Servant as an "admirable but arid fate." To participate in the great game of world politics was "immensely stimulating," but it also "drained away one's other interests, leaving behind it a sediment of dissatisfaction."[24] Ritchie was an exception. I detected very little of such a sediment amongst the men I knew in those heady days.

What were they dedicated to? In part, it was to a brave new world. Pearson and Reid were especially susceptible to the vision of world federalism, a vision that they did not lose even though the Cold War dashed any hope of early success. But this was probably not the main motivation of most of the civilian soldiers in the East Block. The presence among them of so many historians has already been noted. Most Canadian historians had trained their students to believe in the progress of "colony to nation," and it was as nation-builders that Canadian diplomats saw themselves, shaping the profile of a new actor on the world stage. If they could also be builders of a new world order, so much the better. They were fortunate that a more or less united public opinion stood behind them, giving a French-Canadian Prime Minister impressive support.

Dean Rusk, an American Secretary of State in the 1960s, who joined the US foreign service at about this time, has observed that "the major problem facing bureaucracy is ... the evasion of responsibility; bureaucrats are very reluctant to take action."[25] Not so in the East Block of the late 1940s. These bureaucrats were only too ready to act. What problems did they perceive were waiting to be tackled in the wider world?

CHAPTER TWO

The Wider World in 1948

The Cold War

LESTER PEARSON HAD cultivated American journalists when he lived in Washington, especially Walter Lippmann, the influential columnist, and James Reston of the *New York Times*. When Lippmann coined the term "cold war" Pearson was quick to take notice. As Secretary of State he was sensitive to every nuance and change of pace in the White House and State Department, and Hume Wrong, the Ambassador, supplied the hard information he needed. Norman Robertson in London knew what the British Foreign Office was thinking, and in any event the Dominions Office (soon to become the Commonwealth Relations Office) circulated to Canada and to other dominions the texts of key British papers on world affairs, a practice that continued for a decade or more. It was not surprising therefore that the view in London or Washington heavily influenced Canadian thinking, all the more so because there were still few Canadian missions outside Europe and Latin America, and even fewer Canadian newspaper correspondents abroad. The missions in Europe were small, and, apart from London and Paris, relatively new. General Georges Vanier in Paris was in close touch with French opinion, but in Moscow the respected Canadian Ambassador, Dana Wilgress, had been withdrawn in 1947 to signal displeasure with the revelations of Soviet espionage in Canada following the Gouzenko affair. It was inevitable in these circumstances that the views of the United Kingdom and the United States on East-West relations should bulk large in Ottawa, especially since these were the only two countries in which the new Minister had served.

The overwhelming preoccupation of these governments was relations with the Soviet Union, and more generally, with the menace of communism. The British had sounded the alarm with Winston Churchill's speech at Fulton, Missouri in March 1946 (on which Churchill had asked Pearson to comment in advance) when he referred for the first time to the "iron curtain." But it was the United States, the awakening giant, that took the lead in 1947 with a program of aid to Greece and Turkey as a bulwark against communism. This would subsequently be extended to all of Western Europe in the Marshall Plan. President Truman sounded the note that was to govern American policies for many years in a message to Congress on 12 March: "I believe that it must be the policy of the United States to support free peoples who are resisting attempted subjugation by armed minorities or by outside pressures."[1] Truman had Greece and Turkey in mind, with the Soviet Union as the source of "outside pressures," but the policy appeared to be open-ended, and it could and would be applied in later years to regions as far apart as Southeast Asia and Central America. The appearance four months later of an unsigned article in the journal *Foreign Affairs* entitled "The Sources of Soviet Conduct" and attributed at once to George Kennan, head of the Policy Planning Staff in the State Department, reinforced the Truman message by calling for "a long-term, patient but firm and vigilant containment of Russian expansive tendencies." Such a commitment seemed to imply a military blockade of the Soviet empire — an interpretation that Kennan later said he did not intend.[2] Subsequent events, particularly the imposition of Communist party rule in Czechoslovakia in Febuary 1948 and the Soviet blockade of Berlin that summer, were regarded in both Washington and Ottawa as ominous evidence of the pressures and tendencies to which such doctrines had pointed. There was no question of American capacity to lead the way in response; its share of world product was well over 30 per cent and of world manufactures over 40 per cent at the time.[3]

The British were more than willing to follow the American lead and did what they could to encourage it. The Labour government elected in 1945 was led by two men, Clement Attlee and Ernest Bevin, who were acutely aware of the communist challenge to social democracy on the

Continent and were determined to help beat it back. Bevin's view in early 1947 was that "the present rulers of Russia ... believe that they have a mission to work for a Communist world," to be achieved by infiltration rather than war.[4] By the end of the year he was considering how to bring about an association of the Western democracies. Gladwyn Jebb, one of his chief advisers in the Foreign Office, believed that, without US aid, Western Europe would have become increasingly subservient to the Soviet Union. Neither the British nor the Americans thought that war was imminent in early 1948. Rather they feared an erosion of European morale and will to resist the process of infiltration. They did not accept or even consider the view that Soviet policy might be motivated as much by fear of the "capitalist" world as by any real intention, as distinct from ideological conviction, to overthrow it. Writing in 1952, Arnold Toynbee expounded this thesis for Soviet behaviour: "The unhappy truth was that a mutual suspicion gave birth on both sides to acts which seemed as legitimately defensive to the party that took them as they seemed provocatively offensive from the other party's point of view. In this atmosphere, one act provoked another in a vicious circle."[5] But this was not a popular explanation in 1948 and it is doubtful whether any democratic government that espoused it could have remained in power.

One person who did incline to the insecurity explanation of Soviet behaviour was Dana Wilgress, who had served in the Soviet Union as a trade commissioner from 1916 to 1919, before returning in 1942 as Ambassador. He was therefore well-qualified to perceive behind communist rhetoric and Stalinist bravado the enduring qualities of the Russian character ("Soviet Man" was a waxlike figure that was to disappear from the lexicon later in the century). "We must begin to realize," he wrote in April 1947, "that the Soviet Union is not nearly so strong as many people believe and that they need our help much more than we need theirs." He dismissed the prospect of the Soviet Union provoking a major war in the weakened condition it was then in. "Apathy is the only word which can describe the attitude of the Russian people today."[6]* But Wilgress agreed that a policy of firmness combined

---

* Thirty-five years later, as Ambassador to the USSR, I found "scepticism" to be a more apt description of the popular mood than "apathy."

with fairness was appropriate, and he did not dissent from Escott Reid's view, in August 1947, that the best way to prevent war was for the West to "maintain an overwhelming balance of force relative to that of the Soviet Union." Reid was acknowledging, in effect, the logic of the policy of containment. He hoped, with Kennan, that this policy would lead to a gradual mellowing of the Soviet system, but neither could have supposed that it would be forty years before convincing evidence of such a change began to appear.

The phrase used by Reid, "an overwhelming balance of force," was curious. If it was to be overwhelming it could hardly constitute a balance. Perhaps this was simply rhetorical excess, to which Reid was often prone. But it also reflected a tendency in the West to confuse Leninist rhetoric, which predicted that "the balance of forces" would inevitably turn against the West, with Soviet intentions. The Soviet Union might be too weak to initiate war in the near future, but it was assumed that, as the ocean erodes the shore, it would continue to expand its power and influence more or less permanently, and thus precipitate war one day. The only remedy was to build a dike, and this too Reid recommended in a public speech cleared by Pearson and St. Laurent that same month. In it he argued that the Western world, if it so desired, could "create a regional security organization to which any state willing to accept the obligations of membership could belong." In addition, he suggested, the West could create new "federal institutions to deal with international economic and social questions."[7] Reid and Pearson were pointing the way to an Atlantic Community, a vision they were to carry into the negotiations on the North Atlantic Treaty Organization (NATO) eight months later.

While American and British thinking was influential in Ottawa, there were other reasons for the strong Canadian reaction to Soviet policy in 1947–48. One was disappointment in the performance of the UN Security Council, the blame for which was laid almost exclusively at the door of the Soviet Union. Canadian officials had put much store in the United Nations, which they foresaw developing into a world government, a process that St. Laurent described as "the real cornerstone of Canada's policy in foreign affairs." But only a few weeks after this statement he had to acknowledge "a growing feeling in my country ... that the UN, because of the experience of the Security Council, is not showing itself equal to the discharge of its primary task of ... ensuring national security." He went on to suggest that greater safety might be found "in an association of democratic and peaceloving states" where the veto would not apply.[8] Pearson privately expressed the view as early as November 1946 that "little confidence can be placed in the ability of the UN to guarantee security ... this ideal is not going to be achieved for many years."[9] The frustration of ideals can soon lead to anger, but it was an anger that Mackenzie King stifled in public as long as he was Prime Minister so as not to offend unduly the Soviet bear.

A second reason for the strength of the Canadian perception of a Soviet threat was the Reid-Pearson-St. Laurent view of communism. Pearson and Reid had a major hand in the speeches St. Laurent delivered in late 1947 and 1948, which were aimed particularly at preparing Canadian opinion for the creation of NATO. Reid had been an active supporter of democratic socialist causes in the 1930s and retained throughout his career and after a strong interest in human rights and freedoms. His experience at the early meetings of the UN left him with a poor impression of Soviet diplomatic behaviour, and as one of the architects of the UN system he regarded Soviet motives with the deepest suspicion. So did Pearson, and both men tended to regard Andrei Vyshinsky, the flamboyant Soviet prosecutor who represented his country at the UN, as an omen of things to come. Pearson too approached politics from a liberal-Christian perspective that interpreted Soviet communism as a perversion of Christian values and the Soviet Union as a state "ultimately bound to come into open conflict with Western democracy."[10] St. Laurent, the leading representative of a province where the Catholic Church was still a major force in the lives of the people, and a devout Catholic himself, hardly needed to be convinced that Western civilization was under threat. In the fall of 1947 he told an audience in Quebec City that it was "perfectly clear that the Soviet Union wishes to see ... Communistic totalitarianism established everywhere."[11] This was the first of a series of speeches over the next year on the Soviet threat to

Western security, a threat thought to be as much spiritual as it was political or military.

Though still a civil servant, Pearson joined in this crusade. In June 1948 he set out to explain communist doctrine and to dispel the "illusion of improvement in the communist picture" by quoting remarks attributed to Stalin in 1925. He concluded that "the fundamental aim of Soviet policy is to make the Soviet Union strong enough to prevail in the decisive struggle which should result from the next inevitable crisis of monopoly capitalism." While such a dénouement need not be imminent, the democracies had to assume that Stalin was preparing for it and they should take steps to defend themselves, both by keeping their own societies "strong, healthy and progressive" and by forming their own security system. This speech, given privately to a Vancouver audience, was not published by External Affairs, no doubt because it contained thinly veiled criticism of Canadian policies on Palestine. When Pearson reprinted it twenty-two years later he confessed that he "would be more concerned now with Soviet imperial policy than with communist ideology."[12] He was in tune with prevailing opinion at the time, however. That same month St. Laurent asserted that all political parties agreed "that totalitarian communist aggression constitutes a direct and immediate threat to every democratic country." The aggression he had in mind was not a military assault. It was a threat to the "values and virtues of the civilization of Western Christendom."[13]

It may be concluded, therefore, that far from lagging behind in their awareness of a new division of the world into what Pearson had already called in June 1947 "two basically opposed forms of society," Canadian officials were in the forefront of the march towards Western solidarity.[14] Their approaches to the form of this solidarity, ending in NATO, will be considered in the next chapter. Suffice it to note now that they conceived of the Cold War as mainly a conflict of ideologies, partly because they were predisposed to react this way, but also because they believed that this explanation would fit best with public opinion, especially in Quebec. It also had the advantage of blunting any perception that they were about to lead Canada into battle once more. But by putting the matter this way they encouraged the view, soon to become widespread in the United States, that communist or even socialist ideas were akin to cancerous cells, propagated by the Kremlin, and best controlled by the powerful therapy of public vigilance and legal retribution. This view did not take hold in Canada, but it made it more difficult to resist the global conspiracy images that were to dominate American opinion in the 1950s, and easier to justify the covert action policies of the CIA as well as the search for the supposed domestic agents of the disease, both at home and abroad.

Reforming the United Nations

Canada took her seat for a two-year term at the Security Council table on 1 January 1948. This experience contributed to the sense of anxiety already described about the "two worlds." But it also led to a new understanding of ways of making the UN effective in the third world, and to the practice of mediation and peacekeeping that was to become a Canadian tradition. It widened enormously the diplomatic horizons of the department, bringing close to home disputes between India and Pakistan, Indonesia and the Netherlands, the new state of Israel and her neighbours, the two Koreas, and the conflict over the divided city of Berlin. An insider at the time has concluded that Canada emerged from the Council in 1950 with a "transformed philosophy of the UN and a new enthusiasm and commitment."[15]

Nevertheless, such enthusiasm was not apparent in 1948. The failure to reach agreement on the control of atomic energy and to organize measures for the use of force against aggression as specified in the Charter appeared to prove the inability of the Security Council to discharge its primary responsibility. Outside the UN there was deadlock on the terms of a German peace treaty at the end of 1947, and in February 1948 Czechoslovakia became the last of the countries of Eastern Europe to fall to a communist coup. In these circumstances St. Laurent and Pearson redoubled their campaign to find other ways to make the idea of collective security a reality. There were four choices: limit the power of veto, wait for the Soviet Union to change its policies, form a new organization, or establish "a limited association for collective security within the UN."[16]

These choices had been in the minds of officials well before the end

of 1947, but it was not until the British decided in January 1948 to go
ahead with talks for a military alliance with France and the Low
Countries resulting in the Treaty of Brussels that the idea of a regional
system of security was given a clear preference. This new system was
not to be "an alliance of the old kind," however, but "a partial
realization of the idea of collective security ... under the Charter of the
UN," as Mackenzie King put it on 17 March, the day the Treaty of
Brussels was signed. He hoped that it would lead to an "association of
all free states which are willing to accept responsibilities of mutual
assistance to prevent aggression." These words were no doubt written
by Pearson. They reflect an amalgam of King's reluctance to think in
terms of a balance of power, and of Pearson's determination to
implement the lesson he learned in the 1930s that "collective police
action ... alone can guarantee collective security," within or without
the UN.[17] It now seemed certain that it was to be outside, although the
attempt was to be made in June 1950 after aggression in Korea to cloak
the UN once again in the mantle of collective action to enforce the
peace.

At the end of April St. Laurent painted a dark picture of the world
situation for the House of Commons. Lack of trust between "two
competing worlds," he said, was due mainly to "the aggressive and
imperialist policies of communism, and an outside sponsorship and
support of subversive communist fifth columns in many countries."
The emphasis was still on communism rather than on Soviet policies
and interests, an emphasis he illustrated at length with an account of
the coup in Prague. Indeed, the situation in Europe dominated this
speech, one of the most comprehensive reviews of foreign affairs ever
made in Parliament. After admitting that Canada's faith in the UN had
been severely shaken, he went on to describe the efforts being made to
organize the "democratic reaction" in Europe, including the Marshall
Plan, the Brussels Pact, and the unification of the Western occupation
zones in Germany. He concluded with a cautious reference to the talks
that were in train in Washington to form a "defensive group of free
states" (leading a year later to the Atlantic Treaty) so organized "as to
confront the forces of communist expansionism with an overwhelming
preponderance of moral, economic, and military force." He gave the

clearest indication yet that Canada would be willing to join such a group, always provided it was consistent with the UN Charter.[18]

If Canadian officials had concluded that major reform of the UN was impossible without driving the Soviet Union out of it, which they were not prepared to accept, this did not mean that the UN was to be pushed to the bottom of the foreign policy agenda. On the contrary, membership of the Security Council was proving, that, much to Mackenzie King's discomfort, Canada was having to deal with unfamiliar and controversial issues. The first was a dispute between India and Pakistan over Kashmir, a dispute that St. Laurent in his April survey said he would have preferred to avoid mentioning and which he treated with the whitest of kid gloves (at that time it was hoped that both would become members of the Commonwealth). He expressed the hope that both parties would "give weight" to the procedure for settling the matter recommended by the Council earlier that month, a hope that was to be frustrated even though a ceasefire was achieved in the summer of 1949. Pearson concluded on his first trip to India in January 1950 that there was "little possibility that any Resolution of the Council would be acceptable to ... the Indian government."[19] So it has proved ever since.

Council intervention in the dispute between Indonesia and the Netherlands was more successful, helping to bring about agreement for the transfer of power to the new republic in December 1949. In both these cases Canada, in the person of General A.G.L. McNaughton, her representative, was active diplomatically, although Mr. King's reluctance to be out in front of any foreign involvement — "I did not intend to have Canada forced into this and that"[20] — imposed a measure of discretion on External Affairs for most of 1948. This experience, however, laid the foundation for Canada's reputation as "a moderate, mediatory, middle power."[21]

Discretion did not sit well with Pearson in the case of Palestine. An off-the-record speech in June 1948, when he was still Under-Secretary, included the admission that "I would have liked in this Palestine issue to have taken a strong, independent stand for what we thought was the proper and right solution, and to have dismissed the British and Americans with 'a plague on both your houses'." Mackenzie King had taken a hands-off position on Palestine, tending more or less to support whatever the British wanted. But the British declined to take a lead, and the Americans refused to give the UN the support required to impose a solution. Pearson supported the plan he had helped to devise in 1947: partition. In the course of the summer and fall the issue was settled on the ground by the defeat of Arab forces, and the new state of Israel entered the UN in May 1949. Pearson observed in his memoirs that "there was little that Canada could do at the UN" in 1948, a reflection of the fact that UN recommendations were not acceptable to either party and that the Council was not prepared to enforce them.[22] But, as in the case of Kashmir, the UN's involvement in the dispute did lead to the establishment of a UN military presence in the area, to which Canada contributed, the first example in a long series of UN peacekeeping operations. If the Charter could not be amended nor the Security Council persuaded to add teeth to the principle of collective security, at least the United Nations could observe and supervise ceasefires and otherwise moderate the quarrels of its members, provided they were not the Great Powers.

The Berlin blockade in the second half of 1948 underlined this distinction. It was not referred to the Security Council until the end of September, despite fears in Ottawa and elsewhere that war might be imminent. Mediation by the six non-permanent members, including Canada, failed. The dispute was finally resolved outside the UN by direct talks between the Soviet Union and the United States. Perhaps it was not coincidence that this happened a month after the signing of the North Atlantic Treaty on 4 April 1949, a treaty that, in Pearson's view, was the best hope to prevent war in the absence of a UN system of collective security.

The New Asia
Mackenzie King met the new leader of India for the first time in October 1948 at the conference of Commonwealth prime ministers in London. Jawaharlal Nehru reminded him of Sir Wilfrid Laurier, and for this reason and others he made "a most favourable impression."[23] No doubt St. Laurent was also impressed, although Pearson did not find him the kind of person "one could get to know easily on first

meeting" when they attended the next conference together six months later.[24] The Prime Ministers of Pakistan and Ceylon also attended these meetings, focusing Canadian attention on South Asia as a bulwark of democracy and freedom "against the forces of disorder and oppression."[25] One source of disorder was the situation in China where civil war threatened to spread from the north and centre to the south, leading to the first evacuation of Canadian missionaries in late November. Relations with Japan remained in limbo as disagreement between the United States and the Soviet Union forced postponement of the holding of a peace conference. So it was with relief that the new team of St. Laurent and Pearson looked to India and her neighbours, not only as members of a Commonwealth now to be representative of much of the democratic world, but as a new bridge to Asia, where Canada as a Pacific power continued to have important interests.

Nehru, however, interpreted the so-called communist threat rather differently from Canadians. According to the official record he told the Commonwealth Prime Ministers in 1948 that: "An anti-communist appeal was not likely to succeed with Asian peoples in view of the extent to which communists had in the past supported legitimate nationalist aspirations. Asian peoples had, however, no sympathy for Russian expansionist policies."[26] This view of communism as a virulent form of nationalism rather than a fifth column in league with the USSR or, later, China, was to influence Canadian dealings with Washington in the 1950s over the proper response to Chinese belligerency. Canada-India relations were further strengthened, and Pearson's association with Nehru begun at the next Commonwealth conference in April 1949, when a formula was found, in part due to Pearson's efforts, that allowed India to remain a member of the Commonwealth despite its status as a republic. Pearson enunciated afterwards what was to become a familiar theme in his thinking: "We have maintained a firm bridge, through that association, between the east and the west."[27] Nehru was to visit Ottawa in October 1949, and Pearson to visit New Delhi in January 1950. Canadian aid to the Asian Commonwealth members began a year later.

A Canadian Consensus

These were not, by any means, the only important subjects to come before the department in 1948. Defence relations with the United States were beginning to preoccupy Canadians in and out of government, and economic relations with the United Kingdom and Europe were high on the official agenda. Negotiations for union with Newfoundland came to a successful conclusion at the end of the year. But the situations in Europe, in the Middle East, and later in China dominated discussion in cabinet, and most engaged Pearson's interests. Above all, it was the negotiations for the Atlantic Treaty, bringing together as they did both foreign policy and defence issues, that concentrated the minds of ministers from the summer onwards.

At the end of January 1949 the Members of Parliament had an opportunity to address foreign policy in the debate on the Speech from the Throne. The government left no doubt of its conviction that NATO was necessary, both the Prime Minister and the new Secretary of State for External Affairs devoting most of their remarks on foreign policy to that subject. St. Laurent once again rehearsed the reasons for turning to regional arrangements in lieu of the United Nations. Both he and Pearson noted that this was a second-best solution, and that if Moscow were to change its policies, it would no longer be necessary. The opposition parties accepted these arguments by and large, although the CCF, on the left, attached more importance to the economic reconstruction of Europe than to military guarantees, and the Conservatives tended to be sceptical of the government's intention to bolster Canadian defences. Aside from one or two newspapers in Quebec that questioned the need for a show of force, the press echoed the politicians.[28]

A combination of factors forged the Canadian consensus on foreign policy by the end of 1948. The first was the Cold War. By emphasizing the virus of communism rather than Soviet strength, Canadian leaders were able to appeal to Canadian values rather than to power politics, a concept that usually implied for Canadians a subordinate role in a military alliance. The safeguarding of Canadian status in the world was and remained a leitmotif of thinking about foreign policy, governing for example the Canadian response to occasional British suggestions for a common defence policy in the Commonwealth. A second factor was the leadership of Louis St. Laurent, a politician who rose above partisanship to speak with equal conviction in all parts of the country, including Quebec, the province most likely to suspect Ottawa's intentions. With Quebec on side, or at least acquiescent, there was no other significant group of voters in the country likely to be dissatisfied with the policies of active internationalism promoted by the new leader. Canada had not yet become the haven of refugees from all over the world that was later to encourage caution in taking sides on sensitive matters. Finally, relations with the United States, always a touchstone of public interest in foreign policy, were relatively benign in the late 1940s. American troops were not manning the ramparts of empire and the CIA was still a novelty. Moreover, Canada ranked high in the diplomatic ledger of the State Department, second only to Britain as a potential ally. The times were auspicious.

CHAPTER THREE

Creating the North Atlantic Treaty Organization: Alliance or Community?

IN 1968, AFTER my father's retirement, I undertook the task of cataloguing his papers for the years 1948 to 1957, when he had served as Minister. To my surprise I found amongst them the first three volumes of the file on NATO, recording the negotiations of 1948–49 in Washington. True, knowledge of these negotiations had been confined to very few people in Ottawa, but were they to remain private twenty years later? These were the official files, presumably the only ones available in the department, although the Department of National Defence must have had copies at least of the official records. I therefore returned them to the Registry, where they were to be profusely mined in the following decade by Escott Reid, the only surviving Canadian official with knowledge of the subject as a whole, and by James Eayrs, who devoted sixty pages of his survey of Canadian defence policy to the drafting of the treaty.[1] However, the first person to make use of them was my father himself for the writing of his memoirs — an appropriate reflection of the fact that he regarded them as a testament to one of his principal achievements in foreign affairs.

This sense of ownership was hardly surprising: Canadian officials made more speeches in 1947–48 calling for a form of limited collective security than did their counterparts in London, Paris, or Washington; Pearson was twice entreated to be the Secretary-General of NATO; and he was the principal author of the 1956 report on non-military cooperation in NATO. But was this proprietary attitude justified?

Would the treaty have been delayed, or taken a different form, if Pearson had not been "present at the creation," or indeed if Canada had taken no part in its creation? This chapter will attempt to answer this question.

Pearson headed the chapter on the origins of NATO in his memoirs "Atlantic Vision." A clue to what he meant is given by the title of the preceding chapter; "Sovereignty Is Not Enough."[2] Disappointed by the failure of the United Nations to develop an effective system of collective security, Pearson and Reid began in mid-1947 to sketch out possible alternatives. They did this publicly, confident in the backing of their Minister, who told the House of Commons in July that such alternatives need not be inconsistent with "the ideals of the world organization." Reid, as usual, was ahead of government policy in some respects (for example, he wanted to convert UN agencies into federal institutions). His key suggestion in August 1947 that "the peoples of the Western world" create "a regional security organization" where the veto would not apply was the precursor of St. Laurent's indication to the General Assembly a month later that some members of the UN might, "if forced," seek "greater safety in an association of democratic and peace-loving states ..." Pearson wrote this speech. He was most reluctant to abandon the United Nations as the main "structure of peace" and the speech went on to refer to "two or more apartments" within this structure as preferable to "wholly separate structures."[3] Reid, on the other hand, had appeared to propose a new regional organization. Pearson had probably been influenced by an article published in the *New York Times* four days before the speech (the author of which, H.F. Armstrong, he knew well) that called for a protocol to the UN Charter to establish a mechanism for collective security if the Security Council failed to act in an emergency.[4] In October Reid went so far as to prepare a draft treaty "to supplement the Charter of the UN," thus returning to the concept of the two apartments.[5] How the occupants of the two apartments were to be decided without destroying the structure remained unclear.

It was the British, however, who took the first formal initiative to create something new. Reid said later that he was disappointed "when I could not get support for Canada taking some kind of initiative" in the autumn of 1947.[6] Presumably he would have liked to show his draft treaty to the State Department and the Foreign Office. But although Mackenzie King had not complained about the September speech by St. Laurent it would have been highly uncharacteristic for him to favour a specific Canadian initiative (there was a virtual cabinet crisis in December after he learned that Canada had accepted membership in a UN commission on Korea).[7] Moreover, Pearson was in New York during most of the autumn, deeply embroiled at the UN in the issue of Palestine. He was unlikely to have had the time to give much thought to the launching of a detailed proposal of this kind. It was the Europeans, in any event, who believed themselves to be the most directly threatened by Soviet and communist pressures.

Thus, when the Big Four failed by mid-December to reach agreement on the future of Germany, Ernest Bevin, the British Foreign Secretary, spoke to George Marshall, the US Secretary of State, and to Georges Bidault, the French Foreign Minister, about the need for what he called a "spiritual federation of the West." He did not propose a formal alliance and Marshall at least was non-committal, preferring to await specific proposals.[8] Bevin did not believe war was imminent. But he did believe, according to his biographer, that "fear and want might combine to weaken resistance [in Western Europe] to the point where the Communists could secure power by a variety of devices which stayed well this side of war as traditionally understood." No doubt he was thinking of the situations in France and Italy where powerful communist parties threatened to win enough votes to bring about Popular Front governments. In mid-January he wrote to Marshall to propose the formation of a union of Western European states to be "backed by the Americas and the Dominions," the first step to be a treaty between the United Kingdom, France, and the Low Countries (Benelux). The alternative was the "piecemeal collapse of one Western bastion after another."[9]

The same message was conveyed by Clement Attlee, the British Prime Minister, to Mr. King but it received a non-committal reply, having aroused the instinctive suspicions of the Canadian Prime Minister about British intentions.[10] But King agreed with the British analysis of the threat. Announcing on 20 January his intention to step down as leader of the Liberal party, he warned that "so long as communism remains as a menace to the free world, it is vital to the defence of freedom to maintain a preponderance of military strength on the side of freedom." This was and is the doctrine of deterrence that Mr. King had long thought might as easily provoke as avoid war. Was he losing his grip on policy as well as power? His diaries suggest he had changed his mind.[11] In any event, the way was now open to respond positively to the British lead.

Spurred by the communist coup in Czechoslovakia towards the end of February, by information that the Soviet Union might demand limits on Norway's freedom of action, and by concern that Washington was too prone to wait for the Europeans to act together before making any commitment to their defence, Attlee proposed on 10 March that officials of the United States, Britain, and Canada meet in Washington to consider the negotiation of a "regional Atlantic pact of mutual assistance" to encompass countries bordering the Atlantic. Meanwhile, security talks between the United Kingdom, France, and Benelux would continue (and would lead to the signature of the Brussels Treaty on 17 March). Attlee said he had two main purposes in mind: "to inspire the necessary confidence to consolidate the West against Soviet infiltration," and to instill sufficient respect in Moscow so as "to remove temptation from them." A background paper was more graphic: "the issue is that of parliamentary government and liberty or the establishment of dictatorship."[12] King apparently agreed, for he promptly accepted the invitation for talks.

France was not invited to participate, a fact for which it is difficult to find an adequate explanation. Pearson was concerned about this omission, but appeared to accept the American view that it might have led to "premature disclosures."[13] Given that the British participants included Donald Maclean, who was to defect to Moscow three years later, this reason must now appear to the French as a stunning example of Anglo-Saxon hypocrisy. But why was Canada invited? There was no pressing need for her participation if the main objective was to obtain an American guarantee in some form to respond to aggression in Europe. Canada had almost completely demobilized and was in no position to be of military help, although her economic assistance to Western Europe had been and remained significant. A clue is given in the memoirs of a British participant who has referred to Canada's "intimate relations" with both Britain and the United States. No doubt the British preferred to have with them in Washington a reliable friend to help persuade the skittish Americans to stand up and be counted. It was a tribute also to the public lead that St. Laurent had been giving in the search for a new security system. Georges Bidault could wait.[14]

Having accepted the invitation, Pearson and Reid had to set their minds to defining Canadian objectives. Reid described the purpose of the pact to be "to rally the spiritual as well as the military and economic resources of Western Christendom against Soviet totalitarianism." Its members should include as many of the European democracies as would join, as well as Canada and the United States (Italy in particular was thought to be in danger of a communist coup).[15] Pearson agreed that the pact should form the nucleus of a democratic counter-offensive and so did King and St. Laurent. King welcomed the signature of the Brussels Treaty, adding that "Canada will play her full part in every movement to give substance to the conception of an effective system of collective security."[16] No one in cabinet appears to have raised objections, given the prevailing mood of anti-communist vigilance, not least in Quebec.[17] In any event, Pearson arrived in Washington on 21 March, where the talks were to begin the next day, unburdened with the usual Canadian reservations about taking orders from the mother country or the Yankees. He did have with him, however, a Reid draft of a possible treaty of no fewer than fifty articles, beginning "We the people of the Atlantic community ..." and including provisions for what Reid called "revolutionary new political instruments."[18] Fortunately, Ministers had not seen it.

The Washington talks took place in two stages. Pearson returned to Canada after the initial meetings to report to St. Laurent and was replaced by the Ambassador, Hume Wrong. Wrong was accompanied by General Charles Foulkes, Chairman, Chiefs of Staff Committee, and one of the few Ottawa officials who knew about the talks. Pearson knew and liked the two principal American participants, Lewis Douglas, Ambassador to the United Kingdom, and Jack Hickerson,

Director of the Office of European Affairs in the State Department who had served in Canada in the 1920s and had been a frequent tennis partner when Pearson had lived in Washington. He also knew Gladwyn Jebb, the British official who was Bevin's chief adviser on Europe and a key architect of the postwar order.

The talks were informal and without commitment; given these conditions and the urgency that the participants attached to the subject, they made rapid progress. No official minutes were kept (the Americans kept a summary record that has since been published) nor did the Canadian side report in any detail on the issues discussed. The available records suggest that Pearson (and later Wrong) had two main objectives: to persuade the Americans to enter into a reciprocal commitment to treat an attack on any of their allies as an attack on themselves, and to include language in the treaty that encouraged economic and cultural cooperation. The British put primary emphasis on the first objective and were relatively indifferent to the second; they were acutely aware that they and their Brussels partners scarcely offered a significant deterrent to any Soviet aggressive action in Europe and that economic cooperation would take time before it made any contribution to their security.

When the talks ended on 1 April the Americans had come part-way to meet the British and Canadian objective of a strong commitment. They agreed to enter into negotiations for the conclusion of "a collective defence agreement for the North Atlantic area" under which each party would decide for itself whether an armed attack had occurred that required assistance from other parties; pending this agreement, however, the President would issue a declaration that the United States would consider an armed attack against one of the members of the Brussels Treaty as an attack against the United States. It was agreed, in addition, that Italy and the Scandinavian countries should immediately be invited to accede to the Brussels Treaty. It was feared by the Canadians, and no doubt the British, that these assurances did not go far enough to give confidence to Europe in the short term, and might not act as a deterrent to further Soviet pressure. As for the objective of promoting economic and cultural cooperation, no mention was made of it in the paper agreed upon on 1 April. But the time was not yet ripe for this aspect of the subject to be raised; it would come. The main thing was that the Americans were moving.[19] Pearson was confident enough to tell Mr. King that the agreed paper embodied "most of the ideas which we favoured."[20]

This confidence was premature. While the Canadians and the British had few, if any, problems in going forward, the Americans had plenty. The restricted and secretive nature of the consultations now began to backfire. Neither Marshall, the Secretary of State, nor his deputy, Robert Lovett, had been directly involved in them. Nor had the two State Department officials who knew most about the Soviet Union, George Kennan and Charles Bohlen. Both believed that the presence of American troops in Germany was sufficient to deter attack. They distrusted alliances and feared they might make a bad situation worse. So did the US military.[21] Above all, this was an election year. Congress was controlled by the Republicans, who fully expected to sweep President Truman from office in November. The Chairman of the Senate Foreign Relations Committee, Arthur Vandenberg, had his own agenda; he was chary of commitments to the Europeans before they had put their own house in order (the idea of Western European union as a third force had strong attraction for many in Washington), nor did he think the Senate would ratify a treaty that obligated the United States in advance to go to war in Europe. The farthest he would go was to introduce a Senate resolution, adopted on 11 June, which only committed the United States to "association ... with such regional and other collective arrangements as are based on continuous and effective self-help and mutual aid."[22]

The delays and doubts in Washington disturbed the British and Canadians. Bevin pressed Marshall to begin negotiations with the Brussels powers, citing the need to bolster French morale and to prevent the Scandinavians from agreeing to neutrality. He hoped that Canada would be invited to take part — "no doubt an agreed explanation of their presence could be worked out between us beforehand."[23] Wrong put the Canadian case for a treaty directly to Kennan, pointing out that this would facilitate Canadian cooperation in North American defence and that a unilateral declaration of support would not go far enough to reassure the Europeans. St. Laurent and

Pearson spoke out publicly in favour of a treaty.[24] However, it was the attitude of the Senate that chiefly preoccupied the State Department and it was only after the passage of the Vandenberg resolution that invitations were issued to the five Brussels powers and Canada to meet in Washington at the end of June. The talks in fact began on 6 July.

The central objective, in Wrong's view, was to obtain an American military commitment to help defend Western Europe, with the addition of "some simple general article which would cover economic collaboration and set up some sort of consultative organ or organs."[25] Reid, however, reverted to the elaborate structure of a quasi-federal union, sending Pearson an amended text of a treaty that was no shorter than his previous draft.[26] Perhaps sensing that this dispute would interfere with the development of Canadian policy, King asked Pearson to attend the meetings so there could be a direct link with Ottawa (the other governments were represented by their Ambassadors in Washington). The result was that Pearson sent no written account of the proceedings, instead speaking to Ministers on his return at the end of the week. Agreed minutes were kept, however, and from these one can piece together the main issues.[27]

Vandenberg's emphasis on "self-help and mutual aid" appears to have convinced the State Department that the Europeans must first show progress towards the virtual integration of their own defence efforts before they could expect American help, and to that end they should also widen the scope of their cooperation to include Italy and Scandinavia. Kennan and Bohlen thought there was little immediate danger of Soviet aggression; "the West must guard against the trap of undue apprehension ... with corresponding excessive military expenditures to the detriment of recovery."[28] The French disagreed. They wanted immediate help in the form of military equipment. The idea of a European army, then and later, was anathema, and negotiating an Atlantic pact would take too much time. The British, Dutch, and Belgians probed for middle ground. Their main argument was that any European movement towards greater defence cooperation would be inadequate, and was unlikely to be pursued, unless North America were part of the team. Nor would it influence the Soviet Politburo, the threat from which the Europeans painted in vivid terms.

They agreed that the United States (and Canada) could hardly be expected to join the Brussels treaty. Some new instrument was needed that spanned both sides of the Atlantic.[29]

Pearson needed no convincing that something more was required. He agreed with Lovett that the Europeans must accelerate their military planning. But this was not enough. He spoke of an Atlantic security system closely connected with the United Nations and therefore concerned with non-military as well as military cooperation. Its members would regard an attack on any one of them as an attack on themselves without this automatically meaning a declaration of war (a point on which the Americans were sensitive). It should also cover means to deal with subversion. Canada could only participate effectively in such a system if the United States also participated. Italy and Greece would do better to belong to a separate arrangement of which the United States would also be a member.[30]

These points were not new. The Americans too wanted any treaty to be tied to the UN and, by now, had abandoned the idea of a unilateral guarantee. The Europeans were naturally anxious that the pledge of assistance should be as tight as possible. But given the public backing of St. Laurent, and Pearson's status as the senior official present next to Lovett, Canadian arguments must have had significant effect on Lovett and his team, who were groping for some formula that might satisfy Congress; and they may have helped to encourage the British, who had taken the lead in pushing the concept of "Atlanticism" in Washington. This, at least, is what one British participant thought.[*]

Attention now shifted to appeasing the French, supported by Paul-Henri Spaak, the Belgian Foreign Minister (and a future Secretary General of NATO), who were beginning to think that the slow pace of the talks was a sign that the Americans were using them to put off decisions on military aid. They pressed for a "guarantee" of US assistance in case of Soviet aggression. If the French had been included

---

[*] According to Nicholas Henderson, "Lester Pearson gave an invaluable impetus to the talks. The Canadians could not be accused of not understanding the North Atlantic viewpoint" (*The Birth of Nato*, p. 43). Bevin's biographer has commented: "It was left to Franks [British Ambassador to the United States], and particularly to Lester Pearson, to draw the conclusion that they had to take the idea of a North Atlantic pact and develop it in such a way that it would meet the needs of both the Americans and the Europeans." Bullock, *Ernest Bevin*, p. 582.

in the March talks these alarms in August might have been avoided, but in any event the "Anglo-Saxons" now levelled a barrage of diplomatic artillery at Paris. Pearson instructed General Georges Vanier, the Canadian Ambassador, to emphasize the historic significance of a security arrangement that would tie the United States to Europe and at the same time give the allies a voice in strategic planning. There could emerge "a real commonwealth of nations."

On his return to Washington on 20 August Pearson attended an informal meeting of the Ambassador's committee, chaired again by Lovett, where he gave his views directly to the French Ambassador (Wrong was on vacation). Pearson was sympathetic to the French desire to obtain a clear, if not automatic, guarantee of American support in case of aggression, but he argued strongly that a treaty would facilitate, not impede, the early delivery of military aid, and that reciprocal assurances were the only basis on which Canada and the United States could enter an alliance. Apart from the issue of the wording of the "pledge," Canada and the United States now appeared to be on the same side of the argument.[31] But this was not to be the case for long.

An agreed paper was finally submitted to governments by the Ambassadors on 9 September. It described "the nature of the problems discussed and the steps which might be practicable to meet them."[32] It arrived on Pearson's desk the day he was sworn in as Secretary of State for External Affairs, and he recalls in his memoirs that "I now had additional responsibilities and an added incentive to do everything I could to bring the negotiations for a North Atlantic pact ... to a successful conclusion."[33] This had been a factor in Pearson's decision to enter the government. He and Reid had written the speeches on collective security that St. Laurent had called a crusade, and now that a vacancy at the top had opened up, the opportunity to carry it on was too important to be missed. The threat of war remained real. The Soviet blockade of Berlin continued through the summer, and as the agreed paper put it, "while there is no evidence to suggest that the Soviet government is planning armed aggression as an act of policy, there is always the danger that, in the tense situation existing at the present time, some incident might occur which would lead to war."[34]

Pearson feared that, without an effective regional security system, decisions might be taken in London or Washington that would "increase the risks and therefore the obligations of all."[35] He had in mind the Canadian situation during the Second World War as well as, perhaps, the recent decision by the United States to mount the Berlin airlift, about which Canada had not been consulted.

The Washington paper included an outline of the provisions that might be part of an Atlantic security pact. The nub of the issue for all concerned was the so-called "pledge"; in other words, in the case of aggression against one party, what exactly would the others do to help? It would not be settled for another six months. Pearson and Wrong were aware that American reluctance to be committed to specific actions in such a case might also be echoed in Canada, but they were more confident of backing at home for a strong pledge than their American counterparts, who must have wondered whether Truman would be returned to power in November. A second issue was that of membership. Again, American officials were chary of extending guarantees, loose as they might be, to countries that could offer little in return. The paper therefore alluded to two categories of members: those who accepted maximum commitments for reciprocal assistance, and those who might offer limited assistance, such as Portugal and Scandinavia. A third issue was that of non-military cooperation. The paper acknowledged the Canadian and (less fervently) the American hopes for provisions in the treaty "to promote the general welfare," but these had to be qualified in the face of European fears that they would prejudice the work of organizations already active in the field of European economic and cultural cooperation. The British were now firmly of this view. This limitation to the scope of article 2 (as it came to be known) was a barrier that the Canadians were never fully to overcome.

The idea of a treaty was now put formally to governments. Most members of the Canadian cabinet had only heard vaguely of the proposal when they considered it on 6 October 1948. It was Pearson's first cabinet paper, and it was perhaps fortunate that Mackenzie King was attending the conference of Commonwealth Prime Ministers in London. With St. Laurent in the chair and Claxton firmly on side, there was little if any opposition. St. Laurent is reported to have said that the treaty might be opposed in Canada "by extremists on both sides" and would require "extensive and careful explanation" (there was little evidence in the coming year of such concern), and Claxton reassured his colleagues that defence costs would remain stable (which they did until 1950).[36] On 28 October, after the members of the Brussels treaty had announced their approval in principle of a North Atlantic treaty, Pearson made public Canada's readiness "to enter into negotiations for a regional treaty for collective security ... with other North Atlantic states."[37] The next day he left for the meeting of the UN General Assembly in Paris (an important date to keep for a new foreign minister), thinking no doubt that the Canadian position on the treaty was understood by his advisers. Reid, who was left in charge of the department pending the appointment of Pearson's successor, was to find that this was not so.

Reid's vision of a North Atlantic federation, the basis of which he wanted to incorporate into a treaty, was not shared by his senior diplomatic colleagues in London and Washington, Robertson and Wrong. With the exception of initial British support, it was not shared either by the other governments involved. Reid reasoned that if the UN could not be made to work because of Soviet policies, a mini-UN consisting of "free" or "Western" or "democratic" states (the terms were usually interchangeable) should be created with much the same kind of machinery for cooperation, dispute settlement, and security. The Atlantic states could show the way by proceeding towards a virtual federation, including an elected assembly. Robertson and Wrong were bricklayers rather than temple builders and knew better from their own contacts what the diplomatic traffic would bear. Their comments on Reid's successive drafts of instructions for the next round of negotiations were acerbic, even cruel, and convinced Pearson in Paris that the Atlantic vision, to which he was attracted, had better be trimmed to essentials before the talks began again on 10 December in Washington.*

* In *Time of Fear and Hope* Reid entitled one chapter "Disappointments and Frustrations." In it he gamely describes the disapproval that his ambitions for NATO evoked from Robertson and Wrong and, under this pressure, the reluctant withdrawal from these heights decided by Pearson in Paris. He wishes he had played his cards better. But, in truth, he had a weak hand.

Accordingly, when the cabinet considered the matter on 1 December the primary objective of the negotiations was simply stated to be "a treaty for collective self-defence among the countries bordering on the North Atlantic, based on continuous and effective self-help and mutual aid," under which "joint agencies" would operate, including a council. It would also have provisions for "co-operative and common action in the economic field." The cabinet agreed that "it would be difficult to support an invitation to Italy," but rejected a recommendation that Portugal be excluded, overriding the view of both Pearson and Reid that a dictatorship would not be an appropriate member of a democratic alliance. Nowhere did the memorandum speak of a "North Atlantic community," a concept favoured by Pearson. He had approved the paper, however, which was sent to him in Paris, and its realism was testimony to his sense of the issues at stake on both sides of the Atlantic.[38]

The diplomats in Washington finally produced the Christmas present of a draft treaty on 24 December. An article on the "general welfare" fell short of Canadian efforts to include strong language on economic co-operation, but the key article on mutual assistance committed the Americans to "military or other action" in case of an armed attack on one of the parties. The main outstanding questions were whether to invite Italy to be a member and whether to include French North Africa in the area to be covered. Pearson and St. Laurent agreed that Italy might be offered some kind of special arrangement rather than full membership, but they opposed the inclusion of Algeria, which St. Laurent thought might cause "political difficulties" in Canada over the "colonial question." The Prime Minister also suggested that the treaty include a provision for review after ten years in the light of the world situation at the time. Both these comments implied that St. Laurent was still concerned about how the treaty would be received in Canada, and he agreed with Pearson that Canada should continue to promote a strong text on non-military cooperation.[39] In the face of adamant French insistence (including a hint that the Arctic islands should be excluded from the treaty area), Pearson had agreed by the middle of January not to hold out against extending the area to include both Algeria and Italy.[40]

A new factor now entered the delicate equation worked out by the six governments. Dean Acheson had succeeded General Marshall as Secretary of State in the second Truman administration and held his first meeting with the Ambassadors on 8 February 1949. Appearing to ignore the work done by Lovett and his colleagues, he reopened sensitive issues that had taken many months to resolve. Pearson and Wrong had known and liked Acheson for some years (the fact that Acheson had Canadian parents although he himself had been born in the United States made for a good start in the relationship), and if friendship is not a guarantee of diplomatic harmony, it can help.[41] Wrong had received instructions from Pearson to press for the strengthening of article 2 of the draft agreement. He was to urge that it commit the parties to seek "to eliminate conflict in their economic policies" and to bring about "greater economic and social justice." It would cause political difficulties in Canada if the treaty were not to contain wording of this kind. Acheson, however, questioned the need for any article at all, suggesting that the point could be made in the preamble. No one else supported Wrong and he reported bluntly to Ottawa that "we shall not get acceptance of your addition." Acheson based his opposition to article 2 on the grounds that it would not receive support in the Senate because it might raise internal political problems, but his comments to the ambassadors also implied scepticism on his own part.[42] Wrong, who shared such doubts, could not have had an easy time. It was not until the end of February, after a direct appeal to the Europeans for support, a word from St. Laurent to Truman during a visit to Washington in mid-February, and a veiled threat that Canada might refuse to sign a treaty without such language, that Acheson agreed to a compromise text. The final text read:

> The Parties will contribute toward the further development of peaceful and friendly international relations by strengthening their free institutions, by bringing about a better understanding of the principles upon which these institutions are founded, and by promoting conditions of stability and well-being. They will seek to eliminate conflict in their international economic policies and will encourage economic collaboration between any or all of them.

If Acheson disappointed the Canadians on the non-military aspects of the treaty, he alarmed the Europeans even more on the nature of the assistance clause, the heart of the treaty. From the beginning, the Americans had resisted the idea of any automatic or specific action on their part in response to an armed attack against an ally, although they had accepted that a military response might be necessary.* Now, Acheson said, the Senate leaders were balking at the use of the word "military," and he wondered if it might not be an "unnecessary embellishment." This comment drew from the Ambassadors polite but firm reminders of the history of the negotiations to that point, including the importance attached in Europe to sending a clear message to the Soviet Union of what would happen in case of an armed attack. Pearson and Reid agreed. They said to Wrong that it would be "better to have no treaty at all than to have a treaty that is so weak and ambiguous as to be meaningless."[43] Acheson retreated. He persuaded the Senators to accept a reference to the use of armed force on condition that each party would take such action "as it deems necessary." Pearson accepted this qualification after reporting to the cabinet on 24 February the status of the negotiations. There would be no automatic commitment to go to war, a fact which would have pleased Mackenzie King, and which suited Canadian as well as American politicians. In the event of emergency, Pearson told the House at the end of March, the government "would immediately desire to consult parliament."[44]

By early March, Norway had joined the talks, and Denmark and Italy been invited to do so, the latter after a long and difficult debate between France and the rest over the relationship of Italy to the Atlantic system. The French employed the same tactics as the Canadians, suggesting that they might not sign the treaty if Italy were excluded. Membership having been finally agreed, a draft text was sent to capitals on 7 March. The Canadian cabinet approved it on 10 March, and Pearson is reported to have expressed his satisfaction, particularly over articles 2 and 12 (the review clause). St. Laurent said

---

* Walter Lippman, the influential columnist, argued that a negotiated solution to the division of Europe was still feasible, reflecting doubts about a policy of military containment that were widely held in American opinion, despite the onset of the Cold War.

that, while neutrality would be impossible for Canada, Parliament would still make the final decision on the type of action to be taken.[45] These three points spoke to the main concerns of Canadian ministers: the treaty would strengthen Canada's natural ties of trade and culture with her historic partners (over 80 per cent of Canadian trade was with Atlantic countries); it was not cast in stone; and Canadian sovereignty would remain legally inviolate. They reflected the goals that NATO should be more than an old-fashioned military alliance, that it should strengthen, not weaken, the United Nations, and that each member should play an equal part in the making of decisions. When the draft treaty was debated in the House on 28 March only two votes were cast against it, both from Quebec. St. Laurent had persuaded any other Quebec members who might have wavered by quoting at length the positive views of the French Foreign Minister and by giving examples of the literature being distributed in Canada "by the few communists who unfortunately live in our midst."[46] After signature of the treaty in Washington on 4 April, Canada became the first signatory to ratify it. Pearson and Reid were right to think that "something of historic importance had been achieved."[47]

It remains to assess the Canadian contribution to that achievement. There was always some ambiguity about Canadian objectives. It arose from uncertainty about how best to implement the concept of collective security; whether, after the stalemate in the Security Council, to create a new organization of all free states, or to build up a system of regional security groups from which a more effective organization to keep the peace might emerge. Emphasis on the first concept led to the attempt by Reid to write a kind of charter for the "free world," incorporating federal principles and institutions; emphasis on the second led logically to a military alliance restricted to the countries of the North Atlantic. Pearson and St. Laurent wavered between these two versions, but their goal was to make the UN work in the way originally intended, thus making a military alliance redundant.[48] A related ambiguity therefore was about the nature of a North Atlantic alliance: was it meant to grow into a community that went well beyond military integration, or was it to wither away once the threat passed? If the threat were as much ideological as military it might not pass for a long time and would require an equally broad response. This was Reid's view, and it suited Canadian Ministers, including Pearson, who had other reasons for promoting the idea of an Atlantic community. But it did not suit as well the Europeans, three of whom (Robert Schuman of France, Paul-Henri Spaak of Belgium, and Alcide de Gasperi of Italy) were to be founding fathers of the European Community; and it divided the Americans, most of whom looked with suspicion on ideas that would limit their freedom of action.

Nevertheless, it was Canadian persistence that led to the inclusion of language in the treaty that pointed to an Atlantic community, although the phrase was not used in the end despite last-minute efforts by Reid, supported by Pearson, to get it in. It would not have made much difference in any event, for Pearson's attempts in the 1950s to convert article 2 into concrete machinery and action failed to rally much more than lip support. Other mechanisms were used to encourage economic cooperation. Article 2 later became the principal authority for the improvement of political consultation in the alliance, an objective that took on ever more importance as the Cold War intensified. The smaller allies had an interest in enforcing club rules, and article 2 helped to serve the purpose. Canada, in particular, could use it as a model for relations with Washington, if need be.

Whether or not an article on non-military cooperation was important for Canadian public support of the treaty is doubtful. The twenty-eight CCF Members of Parliament might have abstained in the final vote if the treaty had been silent on the subject, but it was not a big issue in the country as a whole, except possibly in Quebec, where memories of conscription were still fresh. It so happened that anti-communism was also an attractive platform in Quebec, and the combination of this fact with the liberal-internationalist beliefs of Pearson and Reid made it easier for St. Laurent to give his whole-hearted support. If communism could only be defeated by a better set of ideas, then "no mere military alliance" would do the trick.

The Europeans *did* want a military alliance, and for them the key issue was the "pledge." The Canadians gave strong support when it was needed. The nature of diplomatic credit or influence is here important. Very few officials were involved in the negotiations, and the relations between them were therefore of significance. Pearson and Wrong knew the Washington scene intimately, and one or the other was at the table from the beginning. The chief American official was Hickerson, with whom they had been friends for several years. His views eventually prevailed over those of the Sovietologists, Kennan and Bohlen, and helped Acheson to convince the Senators to swallow the commitment to use armed force if necessary. Moreover, Wrong's relations with Acheson probably helped him to persuade Acheson to accept a separate article 2. Extra influence was added when Pearson joined the cabinet in September 1948. Unlike Ernest Bevin, he appears never to have dealt with Marshall, but he knew Acheson better than any of his peers. Pearson also struck up good relations with Bevin, and Allan Bullock, Bevin's biographer, states that Bevin "always laid emphasis on the part played by Canada, particularly Lester Pearson."[49] Personal relations would have mattered less if Canadian policies had not also been moving in the direction of closer economic and defence relations with the United States. Nor were Canadian motives suspect, as those of the Europeans, who badly needed American military aid, might have been. Taken all in all, Canadian views appear to have had significant, if often indirect, influence on the outcome. They reached American opinion through the press (Pearson was known to and liked by the Washington press) and the pages of the establishment journal, *Foreign Affairs*. Canadian opinions were seldom given directly to American politicians (a practice discouraged in those days by the State Department), but they were certainly known to the Senate leaders.

Nevertheless, it would be wrong to exaggerate the Canadian role. To be sure, they were the first to give voice to the idea of a regional Atlantic pact, but it was the British who initiated the negotiations and the Americans who produced the first draft and set the limits on what it would contain. Perhaps the chief credit for the final result should go to Moscow. Failure to agree on the future of Germany, the Berlin blockade, the coup in Prague, the policies of the French and Italian communist parties — these provided the impetus to reach agreement. No one thought the Red Army would be ordered to march. Rather, it was a combination of communist dogma and political appeal plus the threat of armed support if there were to be revolution that inspired fear in Western Europe. Bevin and Bidault believed that only a firm American commitment to use military force if necessary would deter Stalin from pressing forward. The Americans were sceptical both about the threat and European readiness to meet it. In the end, they accepted the challenge because other alternatives — great power cooperation or European unity — appeared to be ruled out. Their "best friends," the Canadians, helped to convince them this was so.

CHAPTER FOUR

The Colombo Plan, 1950: Helping the New Asia

TWO WEEKS AFTER signing the North Atlantic Treaty on 4 April 1949, Lester Pearson arrived in London for a meeting of Commonwealth Prime Ministers (St. Laurent had decided he could not leave Ottawa at the time and in any case he was not enthusiastic about such meetings). At the signing ceremony Pearson had said: "The North Atlantic community is part of the world community, and as we grow stronger to preserve the peace, all free men grow stronger with us. The world today is too small, too interdependent, for even regional isolation."[1] The Commonwealth now exemplified this view of the world. India, Pakistan, and Ceylon had joined in 1948, their governments representing most of the "free men" in the world that Pearson had in mind. By this, he meant political freedom. The concept of economic freedom was too ambiguous (were there overtones of Marx?) to be attractive to Western opinion, and the idea of helping to bring it about in countries outside the West through bilateral aid programs had yet to be put into practice. For Pearson and his advisers it was above all the poverty and the promise of India and Pakistan that would inspire support for the Colombo Plan. Nehru had published his *The Discovery of India* in 1946. Canadians were soon to follow suit, and a Canadian High Commissioner arrived in the summer of 1947.

The question before the Prime Ministers in April 1949 was how to reconcile India's decision to adopt a republican constitution with an association of which the distinctive characteristic was allegiance to the British crown. The Canadian cabinet viewed India's decision with mixed feelings. Pearson had informed his colleagues that it was important that India remain in the Commonwealth "not only in terms of the Soviet menace but also as providing an important link between the people of Asia and the Western countries." But India's membership should not be agreed at the expense of Canada's own link with the monarchy. Accordingly, it was to be hoped that India would retain "some link ... with the Crown."[2]

Pearson's instructions were therefore flexible enough to permit room for manoeuvre. He was just as much at home in London as he was in Washington, knowing most officials by their first names, although the Commonwealth leaders were new to him. As the junior member of the group he said little in the formal sessions, but he was active behind the scenes and took a large hand in the drafting of the final declaration, the language of which (like Indian English) was sufficiently ambiguous for India to accept it and the others to claim that nothing had changed.[3] He was impressed by Nehru ("a magnificent mind") and described his concluding statement as "the best statement of the conference."[4] Nehru said that democracy in India was threatened from two sides: "first by a direct onslaught by communism; and secondly by an internal weakening, largely due to unfavourable economic conditions ... policy should be directed against this second danger, for it was this which would create the conditions in which communism would flourish." Nehru repeated this analysis to the Canadian Parliament in October 1949: "The troubles and discontents of ... the greater part of Asia are the result of obstructed freedom and dire poverty. The remedy is to accelerate the advent of freedom and to remove want."[5] This was a view of the matter that influenced Pearson when he travelled to Colombo, Ceylon (now Sri Lanka) for the meeting of Commonwealth Foreign Ministers three months later.

The meeting, which opened on 9 January 1950, was the first of its kind and was destined to be the last; meetings of Prime Ministers and of officials were afterwards found to be sufficient for the purpose of exchanging views on foreign policy. It was held in Ceylon to mark the significance of the new, multiracial Commonwealth, and because, as Pearson put it, after his return, "the centre of gravity in international affairs has, to some extent at least, moved to Asia."[6] It took five days to reach Colombo in the pre-jet age, one reason, no doubt, the Pearsons (Maryon Pearson went along) decided to see as much as they could of Asia, by visiting India, Pakistan, Singapore, and Japan on their way home. The visits to India and Pakistan had a profound effect on Pearson's sense of world politics — an effect that went beyond hearing again Nehru's views on the new forces at work in Asia and one that was strengthened by seeing something of the conditions in which people lived. He reported to the House on his return that "we agreed at Colombo that the forces of totalitarian expansionism ... cannot be checked, if, through stupidity or shortsightedness on the part of democratic powers, totalitarianism is able to ally itself successfully with the forces of national liberation and social reform." The answer, he said, was self-help and mutual aid, echoing the formula made famous by Truman and Vandenberg as the basis of American support for Europe.[7] China was now governed by a communist party. Vietnam appeared to be facing the same fate, and there was trouble in the British colony of Malaya. But a second Marshall Plan, this one for Asia, was beyond Western means even if the US took part, which was by no means certain. Instead, the Ministers recommended that Commonwealth governments meet again in the spring to assess Asian needs and possible responses.

This was an Australian proposal, supported by Ceylon and by Ernest Bevin, the British Foreign Secretary, who, along with Nehru, was a dominant presence at the meeting.[*] The Ministers had not expected to discuss development issues, with which they were largely unfamiliar, and Pearson was not prepared to do so. He took part in the discussion of political issues in Asia, dominated by the new situation in China, but his only formal statement dealt with the future of international trade, particularly in the Atlantic region, since Canada was the only member of the group outside the sterling area.[8] His confidential report to Ottawa on the proposal to assess economic

---

[*] Bevin was much loved by his staff at the Foreign Office, partly because of his Pygmalion-like approach to the English language. My mother recorded in her diary, after she accompanied Bevin on a visit to a Buddhist temple near Colombo: "Ernie said to me in the car: 'That just about did for me, it done me up proper.' He had to smell a capsule to revive him."

needs was non-committal, not to say cool,[9] and in his later statement to Parliament he noted pointedly that Canada's ability to help would have to be related to financial commitments elsewhere — in other words, to Europe. Britain, Australia, and New Zealand were not in any better position to offer much help, but all hoped that a plan of this kind would tempt Uncle Sam to join it.

What motives lay behind this first scheme for bilateral aid to developing countries? The British certainly hoped that a flow of dollars into the area (if the United States cooperated) would relieve some of the pressure on their own financial resources, under strain from drawings on sterling balances accumulated during the war. Bevin also believed that "the best way to oppose communism was to attack the living conditions which gave force to its appeal" (the thesis emphasized by Nehru).[10] The Australians were worried about stability in the newly independent Indonesia, so close to their borders. Douglas LePan, who was Pearson's adviser on economic matters in Colombo, has concluded that Canada's "principal motives must be found ... on grounds that are usually called 'humanitarian'."[11] Given the fact that Escott Reid and Pearson, as well as LePan, were inclined to think in such terms anyway, this is no doubt true. Robert Mayhew, the Minister of Fisheries, who accompanied Pearson on his trip, certainly came to think this way too, as his support for Pearson in cabinet was later to demonstrate. But the emphasis that Pearson put on public record was on the defeat of communism. It was reflected in Canadian press accounts. For example, the meeting was projected to be "democracy's answer to the spread of communism in Asia." For Pearson and Reid, democratic values and human rights were pre-eminent. If these were not achievable in conditions of poverty and injustice they would be put aside and other values — whether of extreme right or left was unimportant — would triumph. An Asia that followed the Chinese example would be a threat to Western values. And China's treaty relations with the Soviet Union implied that a communist Asia would greatly increase the threat to Western security. "There is no more important question in the world today," Pearson said on his return from Asia, than the possibility that "communist expansionism may now spill over into southeast Asia as well as into the Middle East."

This was not just empty rhetoric. The official brief he had with him in Colombo was more forthright: "The immediate problem of world peace is the containment of Soviet communism within its own borders." No one apparently doubted that this particular brand of ideology was easily exportable.[12]

This was not the only threat to peace in the area. Pearson was disturbed by "the intensity and bitterness of feeling" he encountered on his visits to India and Pakistan over the issue of Kashmir. He noted in his account of the trip that he had taken the line with both sides that "it was tragic beyond words that the strength and prestige of India (and Pakistan) should be sapped by their inability to settle this dispute."[13] India was spending over 60 per cent of its budget on defence, a fact that the sceptics about Canadian aid to South Asia were to question later. But Pearson rejected a plea from the British to support Pakistan's case while he was in New Delhi. An American attempt to do so had aroused "a violent reaction in New Delhi," and it was not in his nature to take sides in a dispute when passion and anger dominated reason.[14]

Pearson was not overly sanguine about the prospects for a Commonwealth aid program, knowing as he did that the British faced difficult times and that Canadian officials were dubious about the scheme. Indeed, the Department of Finance had declined to be represented at Colombo. However, he had committed the government to participation in the new consultative committee that was to meet in Australia in May, and Robert Mayhew was accordingly appointed by cabinet to lead the delegation. Mayhew, who had had little experience as the Canadian spokesman at international conferences, was hopelessly out of his depth in the view of his principal adviser, Douglas LePan, all the more so because his Australian host, Percy Spender, was determined to reach substantive agreements that went well beyond the instructions provided to the delegation.[15] These ruled out any commitment to promise financial aid at this stage, and expressed a preference for the United Nations as the vehicle for technical assistance to the area. Canada would only consider additional proposals "if it were felt that more help was needed than could be had through the UN."[16] Meeting resistance from others, as well as from Canada, Spender had to drop his proposals for emergency financial assistance and a Commonwealth fund, and retreated to a more modest plan for a three-year program of technical assistance to be coordinated by a new Commonwealth office to be located in Colombo. It was agreed to recommend this plan, costing £8 million, to governments, as well as to prepare a report on a comprehensive six-year program of economic development for South and Southeast Asia to be considered in September.

Pearson and Mayhew recommended to cabinet that Canada contribute half a million dollars per year to the technical assistance program, or about 7 per cent of the total (the United Kingdom and Australia had announced they would each contribute 35 per cent of the total, and New Zealand and India 10 per cent each). Even this rather paltry sum was opposed by the Minister of Finance, Douglas Abbott, who was concerned that the Commonwealth scheme would duplicate, and perhaps undermine, an expanded program of technical assistance about to be approved by the UN, a contribution to which was also before cabinet. It was therefore decided to deduct one-fifth of the amount allotted to the Commonwealth and add it to the larger sum recommended for the UN, and officials were instructed to do everything possible to merge the two schemes.[17] This housekeeping approach to international programs was no doubt worthy of the auditor mentality of the Department of Finance, already troubled by the prospect of new commitments to NATO, but it boded ill for any large-scale Canadian effort to extend capital assistance to the Asian members of the Commonwealth, which Pearson had become convinced was in the Canadian interest. In announcing the two grants to Parliament on 29 June Mayhew warned that "Canada's ability to help would be severely restricted by its other international commitments." He put the emphasis instead on the opportunities for private investment in the area.[18]

When this announcement was made Pearson was dealing with a new crisis, one that was to cast the Colombo Plan in a more intense light. Four days before, North Korean forces had invaded the South. Members of Parliament paid little attention to Mayhew's speech as they sought answers to questions about Korea. Until then, Western governments had believed that the Atlantic area was the most likely scene of attack, if it should come. Now, as Pearson put it in a note to St. Laurent in August, "the Korean crisis has shaken the already insecure foundations of world peace and has shown all too clearly that these foundations are as weak (if not weaker) in the East as they are at the edge of the European iron curtain." He added that it was "more important even than before to do what we can to re-assure the governments and peoples of the East of our interest, our sympathy, and our support."[19] Accordingly, instructions prepared for the London meeting of the Consultative Committee in September were a good deal more flexible than before. But they were still cautious. While they recognized "the urgent need for economic development in Asia and the essential part of external financial assistance in meeting that need," the government could only undertake at the time "to give sympathetic and earnest consideration to the question of participation." There was no substantial surplus in the current balance of payments and there would be increased defence expenditures. Moreover, "the participation of the US in any plan is obviously of paramount importance," and its nature was unknown at the time. Technical rather than capital assistance was the ministerial preference.[20]

Mayhew was again the Canadian representative at the London meeting of the Consultative Committee, but this time he was accompanied by a senior member of the Department of Finance, John Deutsch (who was to become a strong supporter of the Colombo Plan), as well as by LePan. Agreement was reached on a six-year plan for "co-operative economic development in South and Southeast Asia," requiring some $3 billion (US) of external aid over the period. The delegation reported to Ottawa that the development programs of each of the Commonwealth countries in the area appeared to be "sensible, moderate, and realistic," and, noting that the plan omitted any recommendation about cost-sharing, advised its acceptance by Canada.

Officials in Ottawa, emboldened by the support of Deutsch, pronounced the report "a good document" and recommended its approval, although without commitment to any specific Canadian contribution until the intentions of other potential donors, especially the United States, were known. They noted, however, that despite the fact that almost 90 per cent of outside assistance would go to India and Pakistan with a combined population of 430 million people, a per capita income of $66 (compared to $1,000 in Canada), and a GNP that was hardly more than that of Canada, the report had glossed over the money both countries devoted to defence in the dispute over Kashmir. Nevertheless, the governments of the two countries had abandoned "earlier grandiose notions of economic development" and were giving priority to measures that would help "to prevent a further decline in the basic conditions of life."[21]

It is notable that nowhere in this memorandum to cabinet was reference made to the threat of communism. Neither LePan nor Deutsch were apt to see the world in such stark terms. Indeed, LePan had drafted the concluding paragraphs of the report, the last of which read: "And speed is necessary. In a world racked by schism and confusion it is doubtful whether free men can long afford to leave undeveloped and imprisoned in poverty the human resources of the countries of South and South-East Asia which could help so greatly, not only to restore the world's prosperity, but also to redress its confusion and enrich the lives of all men everywhere."[22]

Ministers were also told of an informal breakdown of possible donor contributions to the Plan (drawn up by British officials) which specified a 10 per cent share for Canada, or about $50 million a year. This figure was thought to be too high. But if the United States and the International Bank were to provide some 50 per cent of the total (which the British expected) "the Canadian participation which would be considered appropriate could hardly be less than of the order of twenty million dollars."[23] Abbott was not impressed by this argument. He was especially concerned that India and Pakistan should be spending on defence about the same amount they could expect to receive under the Plan, and he raised the issue of population growth as a second reason for caution. The Prime Minister, displaying the habit of mind of an experienced corporate lawyer, wondered whether the UN would not be a more appropriate organization to deliver technical assistance. After three meetings, the cabinet agreed only to approve publication of the report, and to accept the technical assistance component of the Plan involving Canadian membership of a Commonwealth Council for Technical Co-operation.[24]

The cabinet decision to leave aside the capital assistance recommendations of the report on the Colombo Plan represented a defeat for Pearson and External Affairs. He had introduced the subject on 25 October, when a decision was deferred. Preoccupied by the debate at the UN on the situation in Korea, he had remained in New York when the Cabinet met on 1 November. This was a mistake; Robert Mayhew was also absent and few in cabinet were apparently prepared to challenge the opposition of the Minister of Finance and the scepticism of the Prime Minister. Pearson was warned by his officials that Ministers had questioned the need for Commonwealth machinery to run the program, and were tending to confuse the technical assistance and capital components of the Plan. He therefore returned to Ottawa for the meeting of 8 November and was able to satisfy his colleagues that there was no duplication with UN programs and that a Commonwealth office in Colombo would not tell Canada how to run its aid policies. But again, no agreement could be reached on the capital needs of the area. According to a report of the discussion reaching LePan, the atmosphere in cabinet was "glacial."[25]

The Colombo Plan was published at the end of November. In External Affairs it was noted that, out of sixteen newspapers that had commented on it by mid-December, all but one were in favour of Canada making an appropriate contribution, partly because this was a better way to spend money "in the fight against communism" than rearmament.[26] So it was not public opinion that was holding the government back. Rather it was three main concerns: the intentions of other potential donors, the economic prospects of India and Pakistan, and uncertainty about the purposes and coherence of Canadian aid programs.

In December, the United Kingdom and Australia announced they would contribute to the Plan some 30 per cent and 2 per cent respectively of the six-year target, with Australia pledging $21 million in the first year. These figures were met with scepticism in the Department of Finance, where it was pointed out that Britain was only agreeing to pay back debts accumulated during the war and that

Australia could do more, given its relative lack of other overseas commitments. The Minister was briefed to rebut these arguments when the cabinet met to consider the subject again on 28 December. Neither he nor anyone else knew whether the United States would make a contribution to the Plan, however, and in these circumstances it seemed wiser to concentrate on the political rationale for helping the free Asian countries.

Knowing that he had to convince St. Laurent if he was to win the battle in cabinet, Pearson wrote to him the day before cabinet met. The Colombo Plan offered hope, he wrote, "that their economies and therefore their free institutions will be strengthened." Moreover, it would help to mitigate the difficulties that might arise in any "exclusive Indian-American relationship," given India's sensitivities and the "impatient tactics of the US."[27] This advice was certainly based on Pearson's recent experience at the UN, where he was serving with an Indian colleague on a committee appointed to recommend the terms of a ceasefire in Korea. Relations between India and the United States were bad and getting worse. The advice was also designed to encourage St. Laurent to regard the Colombo Plan as a significant political as well as economic instrument, and to approach it in this light at the January meeting of Commonwealth Prime Ministers in London. It was unthinkable, in Pearson's view, that St. Laurent should not be able to tell his peers that Canada had approved the Plan, even if the Canadian contribution were to remain undecided. This tactic worked. St. Laurent told the cabinet that "there should be evidence of a sympathetic attitude on the part of Western countries" towards the Asian members of the Plan, and it was agreed that Canada would participate in the next meeting of the Consultative Committee, to which the United States was to be invited as well. No decision was taken about the size of a Canadian contribution, the Minister of Finance being recorded as remarking only that it should be "as modest as possible."[28]

The month of January 1951 may have been the busiest and most stressful thirty days that Pearson had ever experienced. At the United Nations, his efforts to devise terms for a Korea ceasefire that both China and the United States could accept had in turn led to competing

Indian and American resolutions before the General Assembly. United States' suspicions of India's China policy grew, and all hope for any early American decision to contribute to the Colombo Plan vanished. Although the United States became a member of the Consultative Committee in February, it promised only to coordinate its own plans with those of the Committee. Canada would have to go ahead in the dark. Pearson's letter to the Prime Minister had suggested that $25 million a year would represent an appropriate Canadian contribution (a figure that, LePan claims, he and Deutsch hit upon after the London conference in October), and on 17 January he wrote to Abbott to propose this amount. LePan drafted this letter and was able to apply to the full both his knowledge of the subject and his talent for the expression of complicated ideas in clear and eloquent prose — a talent which stood out even in that company of East Block scholar diplomats. He began by repeating views about the dangers to South Asia posed by communist imperialism which Pearson had used in public and which Abbott certainly accepted, went on to explain why the United Kingdom's contribution represented a real burden for its economy, and then tackled the argument that a sum of $3 billion over six years would do little to promote economic development in so populous an area. He concluded: "I do not think it too much to hope that, if finance can be found for the Colombo Plan ... and if capital goods can be made available, at the end of the six-year period the countries of South and Southeast Asia will not only have a somewhat higher standard of living than they have at the present time and so will be at least partially immune from the attractions of communist propaganda, but will also be in a position from which a much larger programme of economic development could be undertaken without further inter-governmental finance."[29] This was not to be, of course, and Western aid to the area continues to this day, but Abbott's view that Western aid would be wasted was not to prevail.

Pearson returned to Ottawa at the end of January to report to Parliament on the Korean debate in the UN. He included in his speech a paragraph on the Colombo Plan, putting it in the context of the defence of freedom, and announcing that Canada would make an appropriate contribution on the grounds both of alleviating poverty and of "convincing the people there of our sympathy and our interest."[30] This was the argument he put to cabinet on 7 February when it finally approved a Canadian grant of $25 million for 1951–52, to be made available "only if other contributing countries were providing enough to give reasonable hope that the broad objectives of the Plan would be achieved."[31] These terms reflected continuing doubts about the adequacy of the Plan in the absence of any firm American commitment (and possibly some pique that Pearson had committed the government to a contribution five days earlier). The totals so far pledged added up to less than half the target for the first year. Official caution led as well to the additional reservation that $10–$15 million of the total be tied to an undertaking by India to buy Canadian wheat and to use an equivalent amount in local currency for the financing of projects under the Plan. Neither of these objectives was in fact achieved. Canada announced the grant in Colombo later in the month without yet knowing what the United States would contribute, and India declined to buy the low-grade wheat that was available. Reservations in cabinet were not shared in the country, however, and when Pearson made public the grant in the House on 21 February he felt able to say that "Canadians, as individuals ... wish to contribute to the success of this plan."[32] The battle had been won, and the grant was renewed annually for the next few years without further trouble.

Escott Reid believed that it would not have been won had the plan not been a Commonwealth concept that appealed to all parties in the House and more generally in the country. Douglas LePan adduced a complementary argument for success — an argument he had put to his Minister to use in cabinet — that "it was right for the Canadian government to act independently in this matter," whatever the United States might decide.[33] It is not certain these arguments would have prevailed, however, had not St. Laurent and Pearson come to believe through their first-hand contacts with Asian Commonwealth leaders, especially Nehru, that Canada had a key role to play in building ties with India and Pakistan, all the more so as the prospect of an American-led war with China loomed larger. The attempt to arrange a ceasefire in Korea had badly strained United States' relations with

India, and Pearson, who had been at the centre of the UN debate, was determined not to let the anger felt in Washington give the impression to Indian leaders that the West had turned against India.

This sense of mission had to overcome an innate reluctance in Ottawa to embark on an Asian voyage that might never arrive at its destination. A senior official involved in foreign policy at the time has recalled that the resistance in cabinet to the committing of significant resources to the Colombo Plan was due in part to a sense that the idea of relief for hundreds of millions of people "seemed to involve amounts of a different magnitude that stretched interminably into the future."[34] Indeed, compared to the $12 billion already committed to the Marshall Plan for Europe, the sum of $3 billion of external finance for South Asia appeared to be hopelessly inadequate. In the end, it was a combination of moral concern and geopolitics that saved the Colombo Plan in Ottawa, a rationale that Pearson later described in simple terms: Canada's purpose was "to assist in raising the standard of living of friendly peoples on the other side of the globe whose well-being and stability are of importance to the whole of the free world — ourselves included."[35]

CHAPTER FIVE

The Shock of Korea, 1950

WHEN LESTER PEARSON informed Parliament on 21 February 1951 that Canada would contribute $25 million to the Colombo Plan he certainly had in mind the possible political consequences in South Asia of a Chinese victory in Korea, where United Nations forces were struggling to hold back the Chinese armies that had counter-attacked in early December. On the same day his colleague, Brooke Claxton, the Minister of National Defence, announced that the 25th Canadian Infantry Brigade would go to Korea and not to Europe, thus incurring costs that would be many times greater than the aid allotted to India and Pakistan. Of the two decisions, the sending of troops to Korea would have been the most difficult to imagine in Ottawa only a year earlier, despite Pearson's recognition at the time of the importance of Asian problems. It was an importance impressed on him by his meeting with the American proconsul in Japan, General Douglas MacArthur, as well as by his talks with Nehru and others in Colombo. MacArthur had told him, however, that the spread of communism on the mainland did not constitute a threat to US interests, which could be protected by air power from island bases, some of which would be in Japan. A peace treaty with Japan was therefore urgent. Korea was "not vital to our security."[1]

Nor was Washington worried about Korea. On 12 January 1950 the Secretary of State, Dean Acheson, had said publicly that the American "defensive perimeter" in the Pacific stretched from the Aleutians to the Philippines. There could be no guarantees against military attack for

"other areas in the Pacific." American troops had withdrawn from
Korea in July 1949, and little military aid was being sent there.
Instead, attention was focused on China, now governed by the
Communist Party, and on Republican charges that Truman and
Acheson had "lost" China. These charges effectively killed any chance
that the United States would recognize the new government, and
poisoned the political atmosphere in Washington. At the same time, US
policy towards the Soviet Union began to stiffen. The explosion of a
Soviet atomic device in September 1949 had led to Truman's decision
in January 1950 to expedite research on a hydrogen bomb and to
review US objectives in case of war. Acheson appeared to give up hope
of negotiating agreements. In February he compared Soviet policy to
the flow of a river — "one can dam it or deflect it, but not argue with
it." The dams had to be built, therefore ("situations of strength" was
the preferred euphemism). In March he told an audience at Berkeley:
"I see no evidence that the Soviet leaders will change their conduct."[2]

Pearson was worried both by the signs of hysteria in Washington
over China — Senator McCarthy had burst on to the public stage on 9
February with a speech about "communists in government" — and by
the impasse in relations with Moscow. He had returned from Asia at
the end of January determined to follow the lead of the United
Kingdom and India in recognizing the new government of China, and
the issue was pending in cabinet by early March. After arranging to
meet two of Acheson's senior officials in New York on 1–2 April to
compare notes, he had to conclude, however, that US policy was in a
state of virtual paralysis. The Americans had "few concrete suggestions
to make about an approach to a solution of any of the current major
problems in Western diplomacy." They wondered whether Mao Tse-
tung would be able to keep control of all of China, and in any case
were optimistic about "holding the line against the spread of
communism beyond the borders of China." Recognition was out. As
for the Soviet Union, there was little prospect of negotiation on any
subject, except possibly on the control of atomic energy. Pearson could
not have been aware that this attitude reflected a just-completed study
of American objectives that called for a "rapid build-up of political,
economic, and military strength in the free world" in order to deter

and, if necessary, to overcome a Soviet threat judged to be greater and more immediate than previously estimated.[3] Until such a build-up was complete, negotiation of any overall settlement would be pointless.

Pearson would have been troubled by the policy enunciated in this document, for it relied above all on military strength to secure peace, a strategy he had rejected despite the anti-communist rhetoric of his speeches. On 3 March he had publicly proposed "a great new effort on everybody's part; possibly some new high-level meeting; possibly a full-dress conference of the powers principally concerned ... on all forms of disarmament" or "a meeting of the UN General Assembly in Moscow." He added: "It would be folly to base our policy on strength alone."[4] These were just the kind of generalities that Acheson and his tough-minded adviser on policy planning, Paul Nitze, author of the new study, scorned. Philip Jessup and Dean Rusk, the senior US officials who met Pearson in New York, must have listened politely but no more if he repeated them in private. But Acheson's views were not universally shared in Washington. Some Democrats were pressing for new peace initiatives. The decision to expedite research on the hydrogen bomb had been strongly contested. Nor was President Truman about to agree to a rearmament program estimated by Nitze to cost four times the current level.[5] The imperial presidency was yet to come, but a decisive step towards it was taken in June when the President decided to react with force to aggression in Korea.

Despite the militant tone of the April policy paper, including the opinion that the Soviet Union would have sufficient atomic capacity to launch a surprise attack on the United States by 1954, American officials did not anticipate the use of Soviet military power in 1950, either directly or by proxy, and certainly not in Korea. Neither MacArthur nor Jessup had warned Pearson of any danger there. A State Department analysis of the situation on 25 June, when the invasion took place, concluded lamely that Moscow must have thought either that Korea was more important "than we have assumed" or that a clash with the United States was "more imminent than we had estimated." In any event, Washington was taken by surprise. The Canadian Embassy was told the next day that, while the United States was unlikely to send troops, it would provide air cover.

But at the White House that day, General Omar Bradley, Chairman of the Joint Chiefs of Staff, was telling Truman that "we must draw the line somewhere." This would be the easier to do because, in his view, Moscow did not want war, a view supported by the US Embassy in Moscow, which cabled on 27 June that "Soviets will not engage in war with US if we take firm stand."[6] Truman was determined to do just that. He later recalled that "Communism was acting in Korea just as Hitler, Mussolini, and the Japanese had acted." If not stopped, "it would mean a third world war."[7] This reiterated the implicit assumption by the United States that the communist states were acting as a unit; it was a view with which Pearson only partially agreed. He told the House on 26 June, after the UN Security Council had on the previous day called for a ceasefire and the withdrawal of North Korean forces, that it was an act of unprovoked aggression, but he declined to speculate about what the United Nations might do in response.[8] In fact he doubted that the principle of collective security was at stake, as the President believed. Korea might be a case of civil war and he did not expect the United States to intervene.[*]

He was soon to be disabused. The next day the President announced he was sending air and naval forces to Korea, and some hours later the Security Council agreed that UN members should be asked to "furnish such assistance to the Republic of Korea as may be necessary to repel the armed attack and to restore international peace and security in the area."[9] Since the Soviet Union was boycotting the Council at the time because China was still represented by the government on Formosa, not the new government in Peking, it did not cast its veto. This fortuitous absence would make something of a mockery of subsequent claims that the UN was acting in the spirit of "collective security," a claim that Pearson, however, accepted more or less without question, as did other Western statesmen.

Pearson had been informed of the American decision before it was made and was able to brief the cabinet when it met in the afternoon,

---

[*] Blair Fraser. *The Search for Identity* (New York: Doubleday, 1967), p. 96. Fraser, who reported for *Maclean's* magazine, was present at an off-the-record press conference given by Pearson that evening. This was a device that Pearson used frequently, knowing that he could count on the cooperation of the Ottawa press gallery. DEA, file 50069-A-40 contains a transcript of the conference.

the record indicating that in general he supported a policy of "limited assistance" to South Korea. No objection was offered to the terms of the UN resolution that was to be approved later that day in New York. This, however, required a Canadian response and on the following day the cabinet agreed to consider whether a contribution of Canadian destroyers "might be a desirable gesture." Ministers were aware that the British were offering the same, and they deferred any decision until more was known of the plans of other NATO allies and Commonwealth associates.[10] The Prime Minister was sensitive to Quebec press comment, much of which was critical of American policy, and he was concerned that Canada be seen to be acting under UN, not American, auspices. When he told the House on 30 June that Canada was diverting naval units into the Western Pacific, he emphasized that "any participation by Canada ... would be our part in collective police action under the control and authority of the UN."[11] This was to remain the leitmotif of Canadian policy in the months ahead.

It was a policy that could be justified better in theory than in practice, for while "collective police action" (a phrase dear to Pearson's heart) did in fact take place, it was not under the "control" and barely under the "authority" of the United Nations. The Security Council accepted on 7 July an American draft resolution that established a "Unified Command under the United States" and requested the United States to appoint the commander. The Unified Command was to use the UN flag "at its discretion."[12] Pearson had tried to convince the State Department to accept the terms "UN Commander" and "UN forces" without success, and on 12 July the cabinet had little choice but to agree to place the three Canadian destroyers, which had sailed to Hawaii to await instructions, under the command of General MacArthur.[13] Britain, Australia, and New Zealand had already taken similar action. Of the fifty-nine members of the UN only the five communist members had rejected the resolution of 27 June. Pearson's worries about the UN appearing to be an instrument of American policy were secondary, however, to his instinctive sense that aggression must be countered, preferably by collective action, if the mistakes of the prewar period were not to be repeated. This reaction was combined with so deep a suspicion of Soviet intentions and so visceral a dislike of the practice of communist governments — a view shared by most of his colleagues in the West — that he had virtually abandoned faith in the UN as a guarantor of security. The fact that the United States had acted to resist aggression in Korea and been followed by others offered "a promise of hope for the future ... this time the collective conscience of the democratic world has expressed itself in action and not merely in words."[14]

No appeasement, then, but also no provocation. In London, New Delhi, and Ottawa there was concern about the reactions of China and the Soviet Union to any build-up of American forces near their borders. Ernest Bevin, the British Foreign Secretary, wrote to Acheson to suggest that the Soviets might help to end hostilities if the mainland government in China were to occupy the Chinese seat at the UN, a view also held by Nehru, who feared a wider war if a deal of this kind were not made.[15] Pearson hoped that the United States would make clear that UN action was confined to Korea and was no threat to China.[16] None of these governments, nor the State Department, thought that Moscow would actively intervene; the Soviets might indeed be seeking a way out of the crisis. But they were alarmed at the prospect of a war with China, and, as Bevin put it to Acheson in mid-July, by the opportunity afforded the Soviets "to divide Asia from the West on an Asian problem" — i.e. Formosa.[17] The Americans responded to these appeals on 19 July when Truman told Congress that he hoped that all questions affecting Formosa would be settled by peaceful means. But they rejected any linkage of a settlement in Korea to wider questions on policy towards China.[18]

Canadian Ministers were less interested in these niceties of diplomatic procedure than in warding off pressures from Washington to send ground forces to Korea. The strength of the Canadian army was only a little more than twenty thousand men at the time, and the heart of this force, a brigade group, was responsible for the defence of the Arctic. The cabinet finally decided on 19 July to make an air force transport squadron available for Korea in addition to the destroyers, and to step up recruitment. Pearson was attracted by an idea of the UN Secretary General that an international brigade of volunteers be raised, to which Canada might contribute, believing, as he wrote to Hume

Wrong, that Canada "should do considerably more than we have done." This was also the opinion of much of the English-language press, and when Britain, Australia, and New Zealand announced on 26 July their intentions to contribute troops, it became virtually inevitable that Canada also would offer something more. North Korean forces were then sixty miles from the port of Pusan, threatening to drive American troops from the peninsula. On 27 July Ministers agreed in principle to supply a Canadian contingent.[19]

They did not agree, however, on the form it should take, nor was the decision unanimous. Both Claxton and Howe expressed reservations.[20] Given this uncertainty, Pearson took advantage of his own and Hume Wrong's excellent relations with Acheson to arrange an informal dinner with him at the Canadian Embassy in Washington on 29 July. Pearson was probably aware that Robert Menzies, the Australian Prime Minister, had told Truman the day before that Australia fully supported US policy, but he also knew that the British shared his concerns about war with China.[21] Acheson appears to have reassured him that the Korean operation would not divert American strength and energy from the defence of Europe, that "everything possible must be done to emphasize the UN character of the operation," and that American policy did not imply a diplomatic challenge to China over Formosa. Acheson appealed for Canadian troops in the context of the wider struggle of the free world against the communist world. The American people were now ready to take up this struggle, but it would be easier for them to do so "if all the free democracies could cooperate to these ends." Putting the matter in such terms impressed Pearson — "a very eloquent plea," he observed in his subsequent note to St. Laurent.[22] He received an equally impassioned appeal from the UN Secretary General, Trygve Lie, in New York two days later. He would have been less impressed, however, if he had known that the Pentagon was then recommending the defeat of North Korean forces "without regard to the 38th parallel" (the dividing line between north and south), an issue that was not apparently raised with Acheson. Nor did he report any discussion of Chinese intentions, a point that Acheson may have smothered by his emphasis on the threat of a Moscow-directed strategy of which Korea was only a phase.[23]

Pearson reported these views to the cabinet when it met on 2 August, the first of four meetings to decide what Canada should now do. All agreed that the one Canadian brigade available must be kept at home and that the only available alternative was to recruit volunteers, either to be trained in Canada and sent to Korea as part of a UN division, or to be trained together with volunteers from other countries. Pearson was attracted to the idea of a directly enlisted UN police force, to become the nucleus of a permanent UN force, but this was impractical in the circumstances, and the cabinet settled for a half-way measure — recruitment of an army brigade "to be specially trained and equipped for use in carrying out Canada's obligations under the UN Charter or the North Atlantic Pact." Accompanying this announcement on 7 August were further measures to expand the armed forces and to increase defence production.[24] A week later the recruiting ceiling was set at ten thousand as volunteers flocked to the colours. In Korea, American casualties were approaching ten thousand, but the danger of being driven from the country had diminished.

With the decision to send troops out of the way, Pearson began to concentrate on the objective of limiting the war. Intelligence assessments continued to indicate Soviet caution.[25] But it was less clear what General MacArthur had in mind, especially after he had issued belligerent statements in early August during a visit to the Chinese Nationalist government on Formosa. Pearson therefore wrote to Acheson in mid-August to suggest that consultations be held "among the principally interested Western powers ... on ways of reducing friction between them and Communist China," including possibly the "seating of Communist China in the Security Council." He argued that only Moscow would benefit from a US-China conflict that would create "grave difficulties" for other members of the United Nations. Privately, to Jack Hickerson of the State Department, he worried that the Soviet representative, who had returned to the Council on 1 August, was winning the propaganda battle.[26] Acheson, who had enough troubles with Congress and with the military, may have been glad to use such advice, which he was also getting from the British and from Nehru, in order to fend off domestic pressures. But the tone of his reply on 9

September indicated a certain irritation. He noted that he and Bevin had already discussed the matter and would do so again with the French when the three Foreign Ministers met in New York shortly (so much for Canadian status as a "principal") and, in any event, measures to bring about the military neutralization of Formosa were designed "to permit a settlement by negotiation," not by force. Changing China's representation on the Security Council could not be considered "until after a solution of the Korean crisis."[27]

Before this reply was received, Pearson had provided a comprehensive explanation of Canadian policy to the House of Commons. Mixing anti-communist rhetoric with veiled criticisms of statements by MacArthur and others that appeared to confuse the defence of Korea with that of Formosa, he drew upon familiar themes: the global scope of Soviet ambitions, the indivisibility of peace, the need to balance the military and non-military means of defence, the relief of poverty in Asia, and the relevance to the West of Asian perspectives on global security. He added one new point: the whole character of the UN had been changed for the better because of its response to aggression in Korea; if other members followed Canada's example "by earmarking a portion of their forces for collective defence, there would be ready throughout the world national contingents for a UN force which could quickly be brought together in the face of a future emergency." Here was a key element of his thinking, obscured in this case by the confusion of collective security under the UN with the collective defence of the "free world," but one that was to take on new meaning in 1956 with the creation of the UN Emergency Force after the Suez war. In fact, no more than a handful of states did use the crisis to earmark units for UN duty.

Few questions were raised in Parliament about the political objectives of the UN in Korea. The Security Council resolution of 27 June had spoken of restoring international peace and security "in the area," a phrase that had troubled the department at the time in the context of the dispute over Formosa. How wide was "the area"? If it did not include Formosa, did it include the whole of Korea? Pearson thought it necessary to include in his review for Parliament only one or two principles on which a settlement might be based: consent of the

people of Korea, and a recognition of the progress already made by the
UN "in establishing an independent government in Korea," thus
implicitly accepting a united Korea.[28] By the end of September,
however, the struggle had turned decisively in favour of MacArthur's
forces, following the amphibious landing at Inchon just twenty miles
from Seoul on 15 September, and it became urgent to define what was
meant by the words "international peace and security in the area." If
the "area" was the whole of Korea, how was peace to be restored
without occupying the North and inviting the risk of war with China?
The question had been debated in Washington, if not in Ottawa, and
when Pearson spoke again on the subject on 27 September at the
General Assembly he was aware from American officials in New York
that MacArthur would be given permission to cross the 38th parallel if
necessary for the defeat of North Korean forces.[29] He would also have
been familiar with the text of a British draft resolution, intended for
approval by the Assembly, which requested that "all necessary steps be
taken to ensure conditions of enduring peace throughout the whole of
Korea," a formula that would legitimize military action north of the
parallel.[30]

Pearson's speech to the General Assembly therefore left the door
open for such operations if North Korea refused to accept a ceasefire.
United Nations forces must be free "to do whatever is practicable to
make certain that the communist aggressors of North Korea are not
permitted to re-establish some new base in the peninsula from which
they could sally forth again upon a peaceful people." However,
"nothing shall be done in the establishment of a united, free Korea,"
he said, "which carries any menace to Korea's neighbours."[31] This was
a nod in the direction of China and was no doubt sincere, although it
seems obvious in retrospect that the prospect of a Korea united under
the flag of "Western democracy" would be perceived by China in
precisely such terms. This was India's view, and it soon became
apparent that Pearson's sympathy with this view was to be a more
important factor in influencing his diplomacy than his rhetoric in
public. He rejected a US proposal that Canada be a member of a new
UN committee on Korea to be established under the terms of the
British draft resolution, and he declined to co-sponsor the resolution.

India's Ambassador in Peking was warning his government that China would intervene in Korea if American troops crossed the 38th parallel, a warning made public by Premier Chou En-lai on 1 October, and Nehru feared that the adoption of the resolution would strengthen this prospect.[32] Pearson was in close touch with St. Laurent who agreed that he should try to have the resolution amended to include a call for a ceasefire.[33] But it was too late. The resolution was approved on 4 October by a vote of forty-seven in favour (including Canada), five opposed, and seven abstentions (including India).

There now ensued a curious diplomatic dance in the halls of the General Assembly, the steps of which are difficult to discern in retrospect. My father described his tactics to me in early October as "burrowing, as usual, behind the scenes in order to knock some sense into the more militant Americans." The vote took place in committee and had yet to be approved by the Assembly. Might it be interpreted in a way that gave reassurance to Peking and permitted a pause in the military timetable while soundings were made there and in North Korea? Two of the United States' allies, Canada and the Netherlands, thought so. Even the British began to waver and Bevin asked Nehru to send assurances to Peking that there was no threat to China's security.

The Dutch proposed that North Korea be given three weeks to cooperate with the UN and that military operations be suspended in the interim. They withdrew the proposal after receiving a stern lecture from the State Department about playing into the hands of the enemy. Pearson, no doubt aware of the Dutch initiative, suggested a compromise whereby the President of the Assembly, Entezam of Iran, would forward the resolution to the North Koreans and request a reply; until then UN forces would stay put. The senior State Department official in New York, Dean Rusk, objected to the idea of a pause in military operations but agreed that Entezam should contact North Korea. So, apparently, did Acheson, but at the last moment Entezam was persuaded not to proceed as planned (by whom is not known), leading to an apologetic phone call from Acheson that Pearson describes in his memoirs.[34] By mid-October American troops had followed South Korean forces across the 38th parallel.

This episode discouraged Pearson, leading him to reflect on

"confusion and division in US counsels." And so there was; the military objectives of General MacArthur were incompatible with a political end to the conflict, but his political masters in Washington could not agree whether, and if so how, to restrain him — a fact that Acheson gloomily recalls in his own memoirs.[35] But the Canadians too were uncertain and divided. Escott Reid recalls that, as Acting Under-Secretary, he "bombarded (Pearson) with telegrams ... setting forth the arguments against crossing the border."[36] In his review of events for the House of Commons some months later, Pearson said there were both political and military reasons for authorizing this action, despite the risks involved. But he did not explain how the decision could be reconciled with a doctrine of collective security that implied the restoration of the *status quo ante* rather than the destruction of enemy forces.[37]

The original assumption in all Western capitals had been that Moscow had encouraged, if not actually ordered, North Korea to attack the South, and that China was more concerned with Formosa than with Korea. MacArthur assured Canadian and British diplomats in early October that neither the Soviet Union nor China would react if his troops crossed the 38th parallel. China did not have the military resources to intervene effectively and in his view the Chinese threat to do so was a bluff.[38] Washington and London were less sure of Chinese intentions and attempted, through Nehru, both to deter and to reassure Peking. Pearson, sensitive as always to the discordant voices in Washington, and acutely aware of Indian doubts (not to speak of the doubts of the China hands in his own department such as Chester Ronning), tried to slow the pace of events in the hope that diplomacy would prevail over military logic. But the channel to Peking by way of New Delhi and back was too murky for the diplomats to make a convincing case that China might intervene. After MacArthur announced on 5 November that Chinese units were "in hostile contact" with UN forces, Pearson pressed American and UN officials to undertake some process of negotiation with Peking and to consider a ceasefire in the border areas.[39] Again, military objectives took precedence and MacArthur began the offensive on 24 November that was to "end the war." It led instead to massive Chinese intervention and then to an uneasy stalemate along the 38th parallel that was to last until an armistice was finally agreed in July 1953.

The few weeks after China attacked in force at the end of November were a time of acute tension in world affairs. Canadian anxiety about the future was increased by the almost complete failure of US military intelligence to anticipate events, and therefore by uncertainty about future Chinese intentions. Would they attempt to expel UN forces from Korea or stop at the parallel? What might the Soviet Union do if MacArthur were to bomb China? These questions now had additional weight as Canadian troops were expected to arrive in Korea by mid-December. Alarm increased when on 30 November President Truman said that the use of atomic weapons was not ruled out. Pearson told the press that he assumed "the President would consult other countries ... before taking any decision to use the atomic bomb."[40] Behind the scenes, he took the initiative to rally the support of friendly governments for a policy of ceasefire followed by negotiation on the questions of Formosa and the place of China in the United Nations — policies on which there did not appear "to be any serious disagreement," the department concluded. Publicly, he described his objective as "an attempt through diplomacy to reach a modus vivendi with the Asian communist world." In cabinet the Prime Minister backed him up, relying on his own instinctive grasp of anti-imperial logic to expound the view that "Asiatic peoples ultimately were going to take complete charge of their own affairs and territory, and would not tolerate outside domination and interference."[41] This robust statement of position would not have been generally welcomed in Washington, nor indeed in the editorial rooms of some Canadian newspapers, where opinion on the whole was belligerently anti-Chinese.

Canadian officials foresaw a grim future. They agreed that a limited war against China would risk a third world war and that, to avoid such a catastrophe, it was important to buy time. Negotiations with China were unlikely to succeed, however. Escott Reid sketched out a global strategy for what he called a "warm war," the objective of which was "the creation of a world in which the Cominform empire and the free democracies can live side by side." This would mean the virtual mobilization of the democracies, he thought. Douglas LePan, who was drafting speeches for the Minister, was driven to the conclusion that nuclear weapons might have to be used against the Soviet Union if one or more countries "around the circumference of the Eurasian landmass" were to be threatened again. The general view was that Moscow was pulling the strings in Asia as well as in Europe and might strike before the "free world" was fully prepared to defend itself. Apocalypse was in the air.[42]

It was no wonder that on 13 December St. Laurent endorsed Pearson's belief that he should accept membership on a committee of three persons, including Entezam of Iran, the current President of the General Assembly, to be established the next day by the Assembly, "to determine the basis on which a satisfactory ceasefire in Korea can be arranged." The third member of the committee was the Indian Ambassador to the UN, Benegal Rau, and St. Laurent noted that Canada's relations with India were a factor in favour of acceptance.

The Ceasefire Committee had to square the circle of a Chinese refusal to consider a ceasefire before the settlement of political issues and an American refusal to accept any such trade-off. Pearson was encouraged by some evidence of flexibility inside the American Administration, but concerned as well by the increasingly bellicose climate of opinion in the United States, which the intransigence of Peking did nothing to alleviate. He and Brooke Claxton presented a joint paper to cabinet on 28 December which argued that Western Europe was the crucial front in the struggle against "the forces of Soviet imperialism" and that a war with China must therefore be avoided. But this might not be possible and Canada would have to review its defence program.[43]

Such warnings inspired Pearson to redouble his efforts at the UN to find the basis for a ceasefire. With the help of St. Laurent and Nehru, who were together in London at a meeting of Commonwealth Prime Ministers, he and his Indian colleague (the third member, Entezam, was largely a figurehead) persuaded the Americans to accept a statement of principles linking a ceasefire and a staged program of negotiations that was endorsed by the Assembly (except for the five communist members) on 13 January. But it was a close thing. He wrote to me two days later: "As late as a couple of hours before we produced it I didn't know for sure whether the USA would vote for it," and he doubted that the Chinese would accept it. Nor did they. They returned an ambiguous reply that was not good enough for Washington, but which prompted Pearson to enlist St. Laurent and Nehru to request clarification. Before this was obtained, however, the United States presented a resolution to the Assembly that condemned China for aggression and recommended sanctions. Brushing aside the "clarification" which Peking sent back and which Pearson thought encouraging, the Americans pressed their resolution to a vote on 30 January 1951. It was adopted by forty-four votes to seven, with India joining the Soviet camp in opposition. Canada voted in favour, despite Pearson's doubts about US tactics — "I have done my best to convince Washington of this [to delay] and failed," he told me. Writing to me again on 6 February he commented: "No one got much satisfaction out of the result."[44] The troops got none, for fighting continued in Korea until the summer, when negotiations for a ceasefire finally started, resulting in an armistice two years later. The goal of a political settlement was abandoned, and throughout the rest of the decade war with China remained an ever-present danger.

What were the main factors that influenced Pearson in this complex struggle both to enhance the principle of collective action and to avert a major war? Most of the personae were the same as in 1948–49 when NATO was created: Truman and Acheson in Washington, Attlee and Bevin in London, and, of course, St. Laurent in Ottawa. Wrong was still in Washington and Reid was Deputy Under-Secretary under Heeney. But the action had now shifted to Asia, and given Pearson's "discovery of India" in early 1950, the views of Nehru became of growing importance, as did those of officials in the department, such as Chester Ronning, who had known China since childhood. Public opinion in the United States had also changed. Reluctant in 1948 to be caught up in European affairs, Americans began to regard China in late 1950 as an enemy to be dealt with by force if necessary. While publicly expressing confidence in American good faith, and voting in favour of UN resolutions supporting their policy, Pearson was critical in private of American tactics and fearful that MacArthur and his allies in

Congress and the press would prevail over Truman's better judgment.[*]
His relations with Acheson remained cordial, however, and these acted
as a brake on any temptation there may have been to split openly with
American policy.[45] Both men agreed that the Soviet Union was the
principal threat to Western security and that China was essentially a
side issue. It was important therefore to demonstrate solidarity with
the administration, a stance that also appealed to a majority of
Canadians. The furthest he would go in public to indicate unease with
American policy was to raise questions: "Our preoccupation is no
longer whether the US will discharge her international responsibilities,
but how she will do it and how the rest of us will be involved."[46] Even
raising such questions, however, came as a shock to some elements of
American and Canadian opinion, resulting in Pearson's "first exposure
to public outrage," as he put it to me a week after this speech on 10
April 1951.

Nevertheless, Canada, like Britain, and unlike the United States,
took seriously the Indian view that a political settlement with China
must be linked to a ceasefire if the danger of a wider war was to be
averted. St. Laurent wrote to Nehru three times during the winter
crisis and was in direct contact with him at the London conference in
January. Pearson worked closely with Benegal Rau on the Ceasefire
Committee. Whether or not these joint efforts, designed both to
explain Canadian and, indirectly, American policy as well as to
influence Chinese actions, affected the course of events is difficult to
say. They certainly helped to preserve a constructive relationship with
India that was to be useful in helping to bring an end to the war in
1953. Canadian influence in this respect ran parallel to that of the
British. They too worked the New Delhi-Peking circuit, and because
they had troops on the ground in Korea well before Canada and had
greater military weight all round, they were probably given a better
hearing in Washington. Ottawa and London were the only two allies to
exercise some restraint on US policies (the French feared Soviet and
Chinese designs on their position in Indochina), but they both

---

* He wrote to me after MacArthur was fired by Truman in April 1951: "The popular rage in the
USA is pretty frightening when one realizes that our hopes for peace depend so largely on the
steadiness and discipline and good sense of those people."

believed that in any crisis short of unilateral American retaliation on China they would have to side with the United States.[47]

A principal reason for this assumption, apart from the military logic of wartime cooperation, was the idealist perception of collective security held by both Pearson and the Labour government in London. This perception was shared by a majority of Canadians, and Pearson had a relatively easy time in Parliament in deflecting criticism either that Canada was not doing enough at first to support UN forces (the Conservatives), or later that Canada was too ready to go along with US policies that might provoke a wider war (the CCF). It was critical, in Pearson's view, to keep the United States in the UN and the UN in the United States; it was also important to keep the Soviet Union in the UN. Otherwise, the UN would lose whatever slim hope it still had of operating as its Charter required. True, it had only been able to respond in the case of Korea because of the fortuitous absence of the Soviet representative from the Security Council, but after his return in August the Western allies were determined to avoid deadlock in future. They secured support for a resolution authorizing the Assembly to recommend the use of force in the face of aggression. (They assumed, wrongly, that a majority of votes in the Assembly would always be available to legitimize a UN response).[48] Moreover, if member states were to earmark units of their forces in advance for UN service, as Canada had done, the United Nations would not be obliged to rely again on the goodwill and armed might of a great power.[49] For Pearson, it was also important that Canada not be seen to be acting as a junior partner. The United Nations would provide the cover and the place at the table that Canada needed for self-respect, and it would allow Canada, as NATO did, some purchase on American behaviour. It was in this fashion that the disparate objectives of national self-assertion and international cooperation came together in Pearson's mind.

#1 Pearson presiding over debate in the Political and Security Committee of the U.N. in 1949, before the General Assembly left Lake Success N.Y. for the new U.N. building.

#2 With A.D.P. Heeney, Under-Secretary of State for External Affairs, outside Parliament's East Block, 1949.

#3 Paris, in December 1951. Pearson, Secretary of State for External Affairs, with his British and American counterparts: Anthony Eden (middle) and Dean Acheson.

#4 Opening the General or "Steering" Committee meeting to consider the adoption of the Assembly's provisional agenda on 15 October 1952.

#5 Greeting Eisenhower, then President elect, on 24 November 1952, with John Foster Dulles (far left), the next American Secretary of State, and Trygve Lie, Secretary General of the U.N.

#6 Human Rights Day, 10 December 1952. As President of the Assembly Lester B. Pearson pays tribute to all nations for the year's achievements "towards.a greater respect for fundamental human rights."

#7 With Paul Martin, the Minister of National Health and Welfare, and one of the seven nickle-
plated doors gifted to the U.N. by the Canadian government, December 1952. The panels in bas-
relief represent peace, justice, truth and fraternity in splendid deshabille.

#8 Visit of Prime Minister St. Laurent to Washington, March 1953. (Front, left to right): Dwight Eisenhower, Louis St. Laurent. (Rear, left to right): Hume Wrong, Pearson, John Foster Dulles. Photographer unknown/National Archives of Canada/C-0090466

#9 Meeting of Canadian and American ministers, 1954. (Front, left to right): John Foster Dulles, C.D. Howe, Douglas Abbott. (Rear, left to right): Sherman Addams, Ezra Benson, Sinclair Weeks, and Pearson. Photographer unknown/National Archives of Canada/C 0090453

#10 Pearson presenting the gavel to his successsor as President of the U.N. Assembly, Vijaya Lakshmi Pandit on 15 September 1953. At left is Dag Hammarskjold, Secretary-General of the U.N.

#11 An inscribed photograph from the U.N. Secretary-General Dag Hammarskjold from November 1956. It reads: "To be or not to be for the U.N. force? With deep gratitude."

#12 Lester B. Pearson receiving the Nobel Peace Prize in Oslo, December 1957.

CHAPTER SIX

The Ultimate Weapon: Canada, the United States, and the Atomic Bomb

IN A NATION-WIDE broadcast on 5 December 1950, five days after President Truman stated publicly in answer to a question that the use of atomic weapons in Korea was not ruled out, Pearson warned: "Anyone considering such authorization ... must remember that the fate of the whole world may depend on the decision. The atomic bomb is universally regarded as the ultimate weapon. It should be treated as such."[1] The next day Pearson sent a note to the State Department enlarging upon this view, and on the grounds that Canada had made "a direct contribution to building up the atomic stockpile" (through the export of uranium), and that use of the bomb against China would involve incalculable risks, called for "consultation amongst the governments principally concerned" before any such decision was taken.[2] He was informed by the State Department, however, that the use of atomic weapons was not under consideration.[3] Three days later Prime Minister Attlee of Britain, who had hurried to Washington from London to find out for himself, led St. Laurent to believe that Truman was "as anxious as the Canadian government that the bomb not be used."[4] Doubts remained in Ottawa, nevertheless, and over the next few months Pearson searched for ways of putting into practice the maxim of "no annihilation without representation."

From the start of the atomic age he had been a keen advocate of the international control of atomic energy — "a new departure in destruction and annihilative in effect," as he had described it in 1945.[5] The explosion of a Soviet atomic device in September 1949, followed by the American decision in January 1950 to expedite research on a hydrogen weapon, and then by the Korean war, frustrated Canadian hopes for agreement on the key issue of the scope of international controls. Pearson had no hesitation in blaming the Soviet Union for this failure, a judgment that historians have since questioned,[6] but by March 1950 he was still urging that negotiations be pursued, if necessary at a high level. Yet he was also reconciled to the conclusion that, as long as the danger of atomic war remained, the West should not lag behind "in the development of knowledge and skill in the field of atomic energy."[7] He accepted the premise that atomic weapons were a deterrent to war "at a time when the Soviet Union and its friends and satellites have such great superiority in other types of military power."[*] His main concern was that American military plans might call for the use of atomic weapons without warning to friends or enemies, a concern that he had some reason to feel several weeks before Truman alarmed the allies in December.

It was assumed in the West that Moscow had ordered North Korea to invade the South, and uncertainty about Soviet intentions raised the fear that the fighting in Korea might lead to a world war. Accordingly, in July 1950, Truman ordered the deployment of medium-range bombers capable of carrying atomic weapons to Britain, from where they could reach Moscow and return. The nuclear cores remained in the United States.[8] In August the President agreed to allow deployment of similar weapons in Goose Bay, Newfoundland; bombers flying the polar route from there could reach Leningrad. The Royal Canadian Air Force had built a base at Goose Bay during the war and US service personnel had been stationed there ever since. On 18 August the US Air Force, skipping the niceties of diplomatic protocol, went directly to the Chief of the Air Staff in Ottawa for permission to transfer forty-five medium bombers and twenty tankers to Goose Bay and Harmon Field (where the United States had a long-term lease), along with

---

[*]"Communism and the Peace Campaign," S/S 51/17, 20 April 1951. I have seen no evidence that, at this stage of his thinking, Pearson worried about the contradiction of asserting, on the one hand, that atomic weapons were necessary to deter a Soviet attack and, on the other hand, of calling for their elimination under international control. George Kennan explored this dilemma in a losing attempt to persuade Acheson to oppose development of the H-bomb (*FRUS*, 1950, vol. 1, pp. 22ff).

2,300 personnel, as a "precautionary measure." Eleven atomic weapons, minus their nuclear components, would be needed at Goose Bay (each bomber could only carry one such weapon in this early dawn of the nuclear age). Permission was granted at once by the Defence Minister, Brooke Claxton, (apparently after consulting the Prime Minister) for the bomber group to remain six weeks at Goose Bay, which it did.

The urgency of the request and the prompt response of Claxton may have been related to United States military concern about the consequences for American-Soviet relations if, as seemed possible at the time, American troops were pushed out of Korea. In any event, there were no proper storage facilities for atomic weapons at Goose Bay and in October the State Department formally requested that the United States be allowed to build them, it being explained to the worried Canadians that "Goose would be the principal Strategic Air Command advance assault base" in case of war. The cabinet agreed, provided that there would be no storage of "special weapons" at the base without the express approval of the Canadian government.

Pearson was in New York during most of that autumn, but he was present at the cabinet meeting in October and is recorded as expressing concern that the United States should be sending ever more service personnel to Canada for defence purposes when Canada was on the verge of sending its own forces to help defend Europe. This was to be a consistent theme in his thinking about defence policy, underlining the anti-colonial instinct which his time in London and his experience of Canada's junior status before and during the war had reinforced. St. Laurent correctly pointed out that defence was a collective undertaking and that strategic bombing was a US responsibility.[9] However, it was also true that, if Canada was to provide an "advance assault base," the government had some right to take part in the planning for any assault that might take place. Strategic Air Command's plans for Goose Bay were to energize the Canadian quest for some kind of atomic defence partnership with the United States, which Truman's offhand remark at the end of November had brought into the open.

British and Canadian requests to be consulted before any American decision was made to use atomic weapons based on their territories created a dilemma for Washington. To give third parties an implied veto on US policy in so vital a matter was politically impossible. If the national security of the United States was at stake, any decision to use atomic weapons would be made by the President. The most the administration could promise after Canadian inquiries in December 1950 would be consultations on "the developing international situation and the military measures which it called for."[10] On the other hand, the United States needed the consent of the United Kingdom and Canada to deploy forces, including bombers capable of carrying atomic weapons, on their territory. In the case of Canada, the State Department was anxious to establish a more acceptable procedure than that which had been used in August 1950, and it proposed in early 1951 that a general or "canopy" agreement be negotiated to govern the movement of SAC aircraft and the prior storage of atomic weapons at Goose Bay and at Harmon Field.[11]

This proposal proved to be unworkable. Pearson and Claxton had accepted US responsibility for strategic bombing, but they also believed that Canada should insist on diplomatic notification, and thus consultation, before "any movement of nuclear components over Canadian territory." Pearson doubted that Canada could object to a request for the use of Goose Bay in an emergency, but he was not prepared to write a blank cheque.[12] Canada would ask to be consulted therefore about any operation in or over Canada involving the nuclear components of atomic weapons — that is, storage, overflights, and strikes, the only exception being "in the event of a major, outright Soviet attack against continental North America." To this end, Canada would also accept a US invitation to hold regular meetings with American officials "on developments in the world situation which might necessitate the use of atomic weapons." Such meetings were already being held with the British, who had tried and failed to obtain a written "consent" agreement with Washington on the use of SAC aircraft based in Britain.[13] So it proved with Canada. No formula could be found to reconcile the interests of both countries, and in the end Pearson concluded that it was less important to have a written agreement than to use Canadian influence in Washington in advance of contingencies that might lead to war.[14]

The State Department hoped that discussions of this kind "would help form a common view as to what conditions and situations would compel the three nations to accept a Soviet challenge of war," perhaps leading to "machinery and tentative conclusions," but it preferred to meet its allies separately, not together, and only when circumstances appeared to warrant a meeting. No such meetings were apparently planned with France or other allies, presumably because SAC did not require facilities on their territories.[15] Pearson, however, was eager to accept the opportunity to explore American thinking on so important a subject, and arranged to meet Acheson in mid-June 1951. He was worried about the state of American public opinion, particularly a tendency "to accept the atomic bomb as merely another weapon." So was the Prime Minister. He remarked to cabinet in May that the US military appeared to be preparing for a general war.[16]

In Washington Pearson first reiterated the view that, for political reasons, Canada must reserve its position as to the use of its territory for strategic bombing purposes, and therefore that requests to deploy such weapons in Canada must be made through diplomatic channels. Acheson did not object, apparently confident, as he put it later that day to General Marshall, Secretary of Defense, that "Canadian consent to the use of its territory for atomic strikes would be speedily forthcoming" in the event of a Soviet attack on any NATO country or "in any other situation that would lead to global war." It is doubtful that Pearson would have given such sweeping assurances, although he would certainly have explained that in the case of a massive Soviet attack on Western Europe, Canada would not stand in the way of American retaliation.[17]

The rest of the discussion, which lasted less than two hours, invites scepticism about the value of consultations on this topic. Barring a direct attack on North America or Western Europe, how was one to say in advance that particular circumstances might or might not justify a decision to engage in a general war? A senior American official is reported to have said, for example, that, while atomic weapons would only be used against Soviet forces, there might be exceptions if their use could serve to "localize" the conflict; an attack on Yugoslavia, now at odds with its Communist neighbours, might be such a case. This official wondered as well if the bombing of China might serve "as a catalyst for revolt." Pearson hoped there would be time to issue public warnings of any intention to use atomic weapons and was told that "in most situations" this would be feasible. Pearson and Wrong worried about the risks of provocation. Would the rearmament of Germany and Japan lead to the Soviet use of force? Was an atomic build-up compatible with the goal of the international control of atomic energy? They were concerned too that inflexible American policies towards Peking would drive China further into the Soviet camp. To such queries the Americans returned firm answers: risks had to be taken, Moscow was not interested in serious negotiations although Stalin didn't want war, and China was a lost cause anyway. The Canadians must have left the meeting in a sombre mood.[18]

That they did so is suggested by the fact that Wrong and Ignatieff* held two more meetings with Paul Nitze, head of the Policy Planning Staff, the following month, after which there was a seven-month hiatus. Wrong again raised questions. Would the forthcoming peace treaty with Japan lead to new American-Soviet tensions? Was it wise to recommend the inclusion of Turkey in NATO, and to hold military talks with Spain? What about tensions between India and Pakistan? Nitze brushed aside these queries (one imagines him in the role of impatient school master). Operating on the premise he had articulated in 1950 that only American military power would deter Soviet aggression, he defended all measures that would help to strengthen this power. As for India and Pakistan, he expressed little interest; they were on the sidelines of the Cold War. Both sides did agree that allied forces must remain on alert in Korea despite the opening of armistice talks.

Wrong was no doubt encouraged to hear at the second round of these talks at the end of July that there would be no request to store nuclear weapons at Goose Bay in 1951 because the facilities for their storage would not be ready, although clearances for overflights "in connection with UK deployment" would be necessary.[19] The storage issue was still under discussion by the end of the year, but on a related

* George Ignatieff was then an officer at the Washington Embassy. He had previously served at the United Nations, where he had worked on atomic issues. He entitled his memoirs *The Making of a Peacemonger* (Toronto: UTP, 1985).

issue there was agreement: SAC overflights could be cleared through
military channels, provided these were not offensive missions from
bases in Canada. In the latter case prior consent would be required.[20]
As it turned out, the question of the deployment of nuclear weapons at
Goose Bay faded away, although SAC was given permission to station
bombers there after the signature of a twenty-year lease to part of the
facility in December 1952. The issue was not resolved until 1963,
when permission was finally granted to store nuclear weapons on
Canadian soil. In any case, the importance of Goose Bay as a strategic
base gradually diminished over the course of the decade as longer-
range aircraft entered the US inventory.

After talks on a Korean ceasefire opened in July 1951, East-West
tensions began to ease. Pearson was in regular contact with Acheson at
meetings of the NATO Council, where they were more concerned with
settling differences between France and Germany over German
rearmament than with Soviet intentions. Only two more meetings of
consultation took place during Acheson's term of office (neither of
which he attended), and after the last meeting Wrong was cited
approvingly by the American secretary as concluding that they had
been useful "in proving that the US was not trigger happy." Students of
the Truman presidency have generally accepted this verdict, at least in
respect of nuclear weapons.[21] Pearson accepted it as well, although he
worried that the advent of the 1952 presidential election campaign
could lead to the taking of greater risks. The danger of war with the
Soviet Union was ever-present, despite the generally agreed judgment
that Stalin would not deliberately provoke a conflict. The situation in
Korea remained tense, Berlin was a possible flashpoint, and there were
gathering clouds over Indochina, where French efforts to put out the
fire of rebellion in North Vietnam were failing. Moreover, a new factor
now entered the calculus of military planning, and complicated the
designs of statesmen: tactical atomic weapons.

At their last formal meeting, in September 1952, Acheson told
Pearson that he regretted a developing British tendency to look
forward to the introduction into Europe of tactical atomic weapons as
a way of reducing defence costs, but he was certainly not ready to
forswear the use of American weapons of this kind if and when

necessary.[22] Nor was Pearson. The dilemma facing the NATO allies was that the military requirements for conventional defence against a worst case scenario of Soviet aggression in Europe imposed economic costs that they were reluctant to meet without taking into account the "atomic element," an accounting that only the Americans could make for them. The British justified their own research on nuclear weapons on the grounds that this was one way to influence US military strategy. There were, of course, other grounds, such as national pride, which British spokesmen thought best not to emphasize.[23] Canada had rejected this option, and Pearson's only recourse was to try to convince Washington to consult the allies, together or separately, about its contingency plans. Canada's strategic importance for the air defence of North America was a factor that could be turned to advantage in this respect, and it was the dominant consideration when the next meeting of consultation took place in October 1953, nine months after the Eisenhower administration replaced the Democrats.

Pearson had held his first meeting with John Foster Dulles, the new Secretary of State, in February 1953. Dulles had been around the diplomatic circuit before and the two men knew each other, if not well. He noted afterwards: "Dulles is not an easy man to exchange banter with, and I would never be on the same terms with him as I was with Dean Acheson, but we shall get along all right."[24] This was an accurate forecast. Acheson had been and remained a friend, despite his quite different approach to the place of power in international relations. They shared a sense of fun and both observed the passing parade of diplomatic society with wry amusement. Dulles was rarely amused, but he was more sympathetic than Acheson to Pearson's ideals of international cooperation, and less abrasive, if more devious, in his diplomatic dealings. He had to operate, however, in a Republican party that was determined "not to leave the initiative in the Cold War to the Soviet Union," as he put it at this meeting with Pearson, and would instead seek to create "threats to Soviet influence at various points in the world." Such a policy would not always allow prior consultation with the allies, he explained. They would have to rely on "faith ... in [US] peaceful purposes." Pearson's advice in turn to make greater use of the NATO Council for this purpose was not what

Dulles could have wanted to hear.

Pearson also suggested that the two governments draw up a new agreement on the principles of defence cooperation in North America, given the growing threat of attack from the air. He had in mind US proposals to establish early warning radar stations in northern Canada, and to deploy a fighter squadron at Goose Bay. At the same time Canada was planning to increase its airforces in Europe from nine to twelve squadrons and was in no position to exercise sovereignty in the north. In fact, at that time there were only fifty Canadian officials in the whole area. This concern was put squarely to President Eisenhower when St. Laurent and Pearson visited Washington in May where, despite their doubts about the realism of early warning defences, they could only elicit from the President a promise that "the US ... will continue scrupulously to respect Canadian sovereignty."[25] American pressure on Canada to cooperate in building a chain of radar stations along the 55th parallel increased during the summer, especially after the first Soviet thermonuclear explosion in August 1953. Pearson drew the attention of the American public to the Canadian defence dilemma in the July issue of *Foreign Affairs*: Canada had to "weigh carefully the alternative risks of the overrunning of Western Europe by a potential enemy, and the risks of attack by the polar route; and to formulate plans and priorities accordingly."

The American estimate of Soviet intentions and capabilities, and of what these meant for the defence of the continent, was put to Arnold Heeney (who had replaced Wrong as Ambassador in Washington) and Charles Foulkes, Chairman of the Chiefs of Staff Committee, at their October meeting of consultation. Heeney found the American presentation "reassuring." The Soviet Union was unlikely to launch a general war in the next two or three years, it was thought, and might even be prepared "to establish a detente with the Western powers." Moreover, a Soviet atomic attack "would not be sufficient to destroy US retaliatory capability." Soviet technology was improving, however, and it was important to have an early warning system in place to give at least two hours' notice of any attack. The Canadians had to put aside their reservations about building a fence around the north. Nevertheless, Heeney and Foulkes insisted that joint air defence be explained publicly as "in line with the NATO concept," thus appearing to have the support of the allies, and that the issue of Canadian sovereignty be taken into account.[26] This was done when the cabinet decided two weeks later that Canada alone would undertake the construction of the new early warning line, without prejudice to an eventual decision on the division of costs. President Eisenhower could well say, speaking to Parliament on 14 November, that "defensively as well as geographically we are joined beyond any possibility of separation," a sentiment reflected in the joint statement issued with St. Laurent at the end of his visit: "There was complete agreement on the vital importance of effective methods for joint defence."[27]

To cooperate closely on defence of the continent against atomic attack was a proposition that made sense, despite its implications for Canadian sovereignty and the uncertainty of success. But what about offence? Should Canada facilitate atomic retaliation or even pre-emption in the case of a local conflict engaging American interests as interpreted in Washington? Pearson did not know that on 30 October 1953 the President had approved a policy that "in the event of hostilities the US will consider nuclear weapons to be as available for use as other munitions."[28] When Dulles announced on 14 January 1954 that henceforth the United States would depend primarily upon "a great capacity to retaliate, instantly, by means and at places of our choosing," Pearson wondered privately how the allies would react to the prospect of atomic attack on Moscow in case of some local skirmish in Europe or elsewhere. Was there to be a reversion to a strategy of Fortress America, and, if so, was there a danger that "the whole NATO system will be weakened and even disappear?" In such circumstances, Canada too might have to review its assumptions about foreign policy.[29] For their part, the Canadian Chiefs of Staff thought it now "evident that the US have relaxed the former restriction on the use of atomic weapons and are now planning their use in any type of military action."[30]

This appraisal overlooked two important players in the decision-making process: the President and the allies. Eisenhower was disposed to be cautious, despite the new doctrine. As for the allies, Pearson was one of the first to issue a warning about any go-it-alone American strategy, and he did so in Washington before an audience of journalists. The Dulles reference to "our choosing," he said, on 15 March, two weeks after the testing at Bikini of the first hydrogen bomb, "should mean those who have agreed, particularly in NATO, to work together and, by collective action, to prevent war," and not, he implied, the United States alone.[31] Dulles was quick to react, asking Pearson to dinner the next day. In a conciliatory mood, Dulles agreed that any decision to retaliate with atomic weapons would involve "consultation and agreement with allies, especially those whose territory and cooperation would be essential for maximum retaliatory effort" — a statement that the US government had so far refused to put in writing. Nor would the United States retaliate "in every instance." The purpose was to keep the enemy guessing. If China attacked Indochina, for example, this would not lead to an American attack on Chinese cities, but if there was aggression in Europe there would probably be "immediate attack by air on Moscow." Pearson found this talk "very friendly and useful."[32] He had not then read an article that Dulles had just published in *Foreign Affairs* which attempted to explain what he had meant by "massive retaliation," and which noted that "without the cooperation of allies we would not even be in a position to retaliate massively against the war industries of an attacking nation," and went on to speak of "collective security and community power." Pearson cited these words when he spoke in the House of Commons on 25 March as evidence of awareness in Washington that "the means [of retaliation] would have to be adapted to the circumstances." But he agreed that the threat of nuclear retaliation "might very well be the best deterrent against war at the present time."[33]

These exchanges provided some reassurance to Canada about American policy. But there remained two imponderables: what circumstances would lead to nuclear retaliation, and how would the decision be taken? The "circumstances" that spring were mainly relevant to Indochina, where the French were engaged in a desperate struggle against the forces of the Vietminh of North Vietnam, led by Ho Chi Minh. Dulles had said to Pearson in their March talk that any new aggression in Asia would not lead to the United States "sending land armies against the overwhelming masses of Asia," but to sea and air retaliation on military targets, "if necessary with atomic weapons." When he spoke in the House on 25 March Pearson referred to the "critical significance of the struggle in Indochina" but he gave no sign of alarm that this might lead to American atomic strikes. He no doubt interpreted Dulles's remark to mean that only significant Chinese intervention in Vietnam would call for an American response. There was no hard evidence of such intervention.

In fact, however, the Chairman of the US Joint Chiefs, Admiral Radford, had been urging the President to use air strikes in support of French forces, and at the end of March he appears to have advised the French military that he would recommend the use of atomic weapons to save them from defeat. Neither Eisenhower nor Dulles had rejected this option at meetings of the National Security Council, but in the end the President insisted that both Congress and the major allies must give their consent before American forces intervened.[34] The British demurred. As for Canada, Arnold Smith, who was then Special Assistant to Pearson, recalls a message from the President to the Prime Minister sometime in April, the purpose of which was to raise this possibility. Whether atomic weapons were mentioned is not clear, but St. Laurent is bound to have repeated the official view that Canada could not participate in any military action not approved by the United Nations.[35] Later in April, while in Paris on his way to the Geneva peace conference on Korea, Pearson was disturbed to hear from Anthony Eden, the British Foreign Secretary, that Dulles was again considering American bombing strikes against Vietminh lines of communication in Vietnam, a proposal about which Eden had "the gravest doubts" because it might bring the Chinese into the war in force, as it had in Korea. Pearson and St. Laurent agreed.[*] Again, Eisenhower backed off, and the Geneva conference was to remove any further incentive for US military action in the area for another decade.

---

[*] DEA, file 50052-40, vol. 19, Pearson to St. Laurent, Embassy Paris telegram 181, 24 April, and USSEA to Geneva, 25 April 1954. I was stationed at the embassy in Paris at the time of these events and recall having dinner with my father that evening, in the middle of which he was interrupted by a message from Eden, who wanted advice about how to persuade Dulles to back off a scheme for US bombing of targets in Vietnam. It was typical of my father that, after talking to Eden, he returned to the dinner table and family matters as though nothing of much importance was happening.

After a further meeting of consultation on 4 March, at which Admiral Radford was present, Heeney commented that he had learned little about American thinking on "world trouble spots."[36] This was hardly surprising, given the fact that Radford and Dulles were at odds over Indochina policy, and the President was ambivalent. Heeney was not to learn much more at the next meeting on 24 September, which the anxious Canadians had requested to probe American intentions for NATO after France, the perennial bad boy, had rejected the plan for a European Defence Community. An examination of new troubles between the two Chinas over the islands of Quemoy and Matsu, opposite Formosa, was also on the agenda. In addition, fresh evidence of Soviet progress in developing long-range bomber capacity was adding to concerns in Ottawa about Canadian defence priorities. The Americans said nothing about how they might react to an attack on the islands and, while they were critical of French policy, they were unable to suggest any strategy that left France out of the defence of Europe, an alternative that the Canadian side counselled strongly against. As for Soviet intentions, they had no reason to think that war was any more imminent than in the past. The Canadians pressed for joint research and development of new weapons systems for the defence of the continent, and complained that they had been left in ignorance of the effects of fall-out on civilians, a menace that the Bikini explosion had brought to everyone's attention.

By the end of the year, Pearson was being warned by his department that US plans for the air defence of the continent, including construction of an early warning line in the high Arctic, would soon raise serious problems of Canadian command and control, especially over the use of atomic weapons for such defence.[37] The introduction of tactical atomic weapons into US forces in Europe was accepted by the NATO Council at its meeting in December, and in this case Pearson was hopeful that the allies could agree on procedures to guide military commanders in an emergency. Outside the NATO area, however, there would be no restraints on the American use of atomic weapons, aside from the vague promises made by Dulles, and Canada could well become a helpless target in a thermonuclear exchange. In early 1955 the situation in the Formosa Strait looked as though it might develop in just this way, leading Pearson to remark that "the most important political problem facing Canada today is the danger of the Cold War becoming a blazing thermonuclear one."[38] His fears must have been confirmed when Dulles told him in March that "if war came ... it would start by Communist air attacks on North America."[39]

The key question for Canadian officials was whether the Soviet Union would support China if the United States struck China with tactical atomic weapons, perhaps leading in turn to a general nuclear war. They thought it probable that the US 7th Fleet in the Pacific was equipped with such weapons.[40] What therefore were American intentions if Chinese troops on the mainland attacked the offshore islands? The issue came to a head in March. A Dulles speech and an Eisenhower press conference implied that tactical atomic weapons would be used if necessary on "strictly military targets"; the Department of External Affairs concluded therefore that "if hostilities are renewed in the Far East the US is unwilling that they should be bound by any such commitment to localise them as existed in Korea."[41] This was correct. Dulles had told the National Security Council on 10 March that "atomic weapons were the only effective weapons which the US could use against a variety of mainland targets," and these might have to be used "within the next month or two." The President was not so sure. A week later Dulles confirmed to Pearson directly, during a visit to Ottawa, that American defence policy was predicated "on the use of small atomic weapons against battlefield and tactical targets," mainly because of the cost/benefits of such weapons.[42] As in the case of Indochina a year earlier, however, Eisenhower never gave the order for such use, in this case because no Chinese offensive against the islands was mounted. The crisis subsided.

There were no further nuclear crises during Pearson's tenure as Secretary of State for External Affairs, except for the apparent Soviet threat to intervene in the Suez conflict in 1956 — a threat that quickly evaporated with the ceasefire. Rather, attention was concentrated on the issue of allied procedures for the use of American weapons based in Europe, or, in Canada's case, in relation to North American defence arrangements. No practical solution could be found to the NATO problem, although for Pearson it reinforced his view that the NATO

Council must acquire greater authority. This was a view he put forward in his report on non-military cooperation in 1956: "Members should inform the Council of any development which significantly affects the Alliance ... as a preliminary to effective political consultation."[43] Canada continued to press the United States for procedures that would ensure Canada was informed in good time of the likelihood of hostilities occurring in which North America might be attacked, given that each side was now capable of delivering hundreds of hydrogen bombs on the other and that one-third or more of the defence budget was being spent on air defence. Pearson accepted that the facts of geography and technology pointed to an integrated air defence system, and some years later this logic led him to agree to the stationing of nuclear weapons in Canada. In fact, his views on this subject had always been consistent with the assumption that the best way to prevent war was to deter it, and if this failed, to limit its consequences.

Pearson was wont in public to paint in lurid colours the effects of nuclear war, but he had little patience with those who promoted campaigns to ban the bomb, and he was prepared to argue, indeed, that the Soviet Union would seek to dominate the world if the United States were to forego the option of nuclear retaliation. He also took a realistic view of the military situation: "We must face the practical certainty that if any general war is allowed to begin, it would become nuclear war, and both sides would have to face the catastrophic consequences." He assumed that such a war would be fought in Europe and over North America. But in a limited war, outside Europe, "nuclear weapons could be put aside."[44] Their use again in Asia "would have grave political and psychological consequences," he commented privately à propos the Formosa crisis. But neither he nor his officials were ready to confront the Americans directly with such fears, and Pearson himself wavered in his view of the use of tactical atomic weapons outside Europe. Thus, in lectures that he delivered at Princeton in May 1955, he thought it would be unrealistic to assume "that these smaller atomic weapons will not be used if there are hostilities, local or general," and he went on to sketch a doctrine "of reasonable or measured retaliation" as against "massive retaliation," and its application to a local attack or conflict. In the latter case, only such force should be used as "strictly necessary to accomplish specific objectives." The principal objective was to prevent hostilities from beginning at all.[45]

Pearson feared that any use of nuclear weapons in Europe would likely ignite a general war. But, unlike George Kennan and other critics of nuclear strategy at the time, he could not bring himself to recommend what became known as the doctrine of "no first use." None of the NATO allies would have accepted such a prescription.[*] They had two main concerns in mind: to deter any Soviet attack by the most impressive means available, and to do this without bankrupting their economies; most were spending well over one-third of their budgets on defence.

There was never any reliable indication in these years of a Soviet intention to invade Western Europe, nor, in retrospect, does such an intention appear plausible. The Soviet people's fear of war was at least as great, if not greater, than that in the West, as Pearson discovered during his visit to the Soviet Union in October 1955.[46] But in the depths of the Cold War no Western statesman could overlook the possibility of accident or miscalculation, nor, at some point, of a change in Soviet attitudes. Moreover, Canada and the other allies had to accept on faith the Eisenhower-Dulles assurance that tactical atomic weapons could be used with precision against military targets, avoiding massive civilian casualties. They had no independent source of information about atomic weapons, nor would US law allow them to gain it until 1954 when an exception was made for the British, who had tested their first atomic bomb in 1952. Not until the end of the decade did it come to be generally accepted that limited war should exclude the use of atomic weapons. Pearson came close to stating such a belief in 1954–55 when war with China appeared to be at hand, but he could see no alternative to the threatened use of such weapons in Europe if war should begin, with the hope that the resulting damage

---

* See, for example, the article by Paul-Henri Spaak, the Belgian Foreign Minister, in *Foreign Affairs*, April 1955. The concept of using tactical nuclear weapons against Soviet ground forces gained momentum with the publication in 1957 of *Nuclear Weapons and Foreign Policy* by a young Harvard professor, Henry Kissinger. He later changed his mind.

might be relatively limited. His doubts remained, however, and he was to wrestle with the tangle of moral, political, and military issues surrounding the use of the "ultimate" weapon for the rest of his life.[47]

CHAPTER SEVEN

Indochina Surprise, 1954

LESTER PEARSON HAD been introduced to the turbulent world of Asian life and politics at the Colombo Plan conference in January 1950. One of the subjects discussed there was the situation in the French colonies of Vietnam, Laos, and Cambodia, making up the land area known as Indochina. In 1949 the three countries had been granted a modest degree of autonomy within the French Union, but in Vietnam a savage guerilla war, begun in 1946, continued to pit the forces of France and its allies in Vietnam, based largely in the South, against the forces (Vietminh) of the Democratic Republic of Vietnam, headed by Ho Chi Minh, a veteran communist, in the North. Pearson told Parliament after his return from Colombo that "our very close and friendly ties with France would ensure our special interest in the progress toward freedom in that area ... in the face of a serious communist menace," but he gave no hint of how this interest might be expressed.[1] The United States, Britain, and Australia acceded to French requests for formal recognition of the new status of the three Associated States, but Canada postponed a decision on the matter, reflecting the strong distaste for these "neo-colonial" arrangements held by the Prime Minister, Louis St. Laurent. Pearson shared this distaste, in part because of his high regard for the opinions of India's Jawaharlal Nehru. Not until the end of 1952 did Canada grant "qualified" recognition.[2]

The main reason for this recognition was growing French pressure on her NATO allies to regard the French military effort in Indochina as

part of a global campaign to defend the West, or "free world" as then
described, and to allow France to divert military aid from the United
States and Canada under NATO arrangements to Indochina. St. Laurent
refused to agree to this request unless it were to be authorized by
NATO, a compromise that reflected both his anti-colonial instincts and
the undoubted fact that the French military contribution to NATO
suffered from the burden carried in far-off Indochina.[3] By 1953 French
efforts were failing, and the new American administration of
Eisenhower and Dulles began to fear that the Vietminh, aided by
China, would prevail.

Dulles told Pearson at their first meeting in February 1953 that
Indochina was "the most critical point in the world today." If it were
lost there would be "incalculable" strategic consequences, and in the
meantime it was a major obstacle to France's ratification of the treaty
on a European Defence Community, which it had signed in 1952. The
situation required that the Chinese be deterred from "throwing their
forces into the war in Indochina"; it was American policy to do this by
encouraging "raids or feints against China" from Formosa.[4] Pearson
did not comment in writing on this strategy at the time. Speaking in
Parliament a few weeks later, he acknowledged a "strategic connection
between communist aggression in one part of the world and
communist aggression in another," but he was careful to draw a
political distinction between Korea and Indochina. Canada had
obligations to the United Nations in Korea but not in Indochina.[5]

Two days later, in Washington, he objected to an attempt by Dulles
to argue that Indochina and Korea were "two sectors of the same
front" in the struggle against Soviet imperialism (as usual at that time,
the Chinese were written off as a Soviet catspaw). Pearson noted that
the United Nations had made no judgment about the war in
Indochina. No government had raised the question there, and until it
did, he suggested, it would seem to be a struggle against "French
colonial rule."[6] Pearson's energies at the time were focused on
negotiations for an armistice in Korea, in his capacity as President of
the General Assembly, and he was hopeful that an armistice might in
turn lead to a political settlement, and even to Canada's recognition of
the Peking government.[7] This was quite a different outlook from the

Dulles assumption that communism, not aggression, was the chief threat to global order. It was also more sensitive to the nationalist impulse in Asian politics than was popular in government circles in Paris.

By the end of 1953 the United States was financing 60 per cent or more of the French war effort, including some 140,000 French and Foreign Legion troops, as well as 400,000 soldiers from the three Associated States, who had been promised but not yet granted equal sovereignty in the French Union. Paris and Washington had agreed on a strategy that they expected would lead to the defeat of Vietminh forces in 1954, beginning with the all-out defence of the fortress of Dien Bien Phu in the north. But in France, opposition to the war, led by the powerful French Communist party, was growing. Why should French soldiers, it was said, sacrifice their lives in a cause that so divided the Vietnamese themselves? President Eisenhower was inclined to agree. He told his advisers in early January 1954 that "the key to winning this war was to get the Vietnamese to fight," and he wondered if they might be more willing to do so if the US army took over their training and if US pilots were to fly the B-26 bombers supplied to the French. He could not imagine the United States sending ground forces to the area, however. Later that month he agreed to the transfer of twenty-two more bombers (for a total of fifty-four) as well as two hundred maintenance personnel.[8] So began American military intervention in Indochina, despite the President's doubts. It was based on a strategic assessment that was never to vary for twenty years, and which Eisenhower approved, that "communist domination of S.E. Asia, by whatever means, would seriously endanger in the short term and critically endanger in the longer term US security interests."[9]

On 19 February the four Great Powers (the United States, the Soviet Union, Britain, and France), meeting in Berlin, agreed to hold a conference in Geneva on the future of Korea and, under pressure from France, to consider as well the problem of restoring peace in Indochina. Dulles had agreed to the addition of Indochina with reluctance, telling Pearson in March that, if he had refused, the French government would have fallen. He was worried about "stability and firmness" in Paris. There was "no determination about Indochina."[10] This was hardly surprising, given the fact that in the 1951 elections about half the French electorate voted for parties that opposed the war. Nor was there much determination in Ottawa, where officials admitted ignorance of any plans for a settlement in Indochina, noting simply, without any of the *angst* prevalent in Washington, that "time seems to be working in favour of Ho Chi Minh."[11] Indeed, when in February St. Laurent welcomed an appeal by Nehru for a ceasefire, there was no public reaction in Canada, even though both France and the United States had made clear they were opposed to a ceasefire until the military situation improved. Pearson acknowledged to the House of Commons in March "the critical significance of the struggle in Indochina," but he did not expect that Canada would "take an active part in discussions regarding Indochina" at the April conference in Geneva, where Canada would be a participant as a member of the UN with forces in Korea. Following this lead, the department advised the CBC international service to underplay Indochina in its broadcasts.[12]

Such anodyne sentiments were subjected to more critical examination in Canada after Dulles spoke publicly on March 29 of "united action" to combat the possible "imposition on S.E. Asia of the political system of communist Russia and its Chinese communist ally, by whatever means."[13] The speech followed intensive consultations in Washington with the head of the French General Staff, General Ely, who asked for urgent American assistance to prevent the fall of Dien Bien Phu, where a garrison of twelve thousand French troops were encircled without sufficient air power to ward off attack. Ely left Admiral Radford, the Chairman of the US Chiefs of Staff, with the impression that the situation would progressively deteriorate unless US airpower could be brought to bear. Given this outlook, the President and his advisers began casting about for a policy that would legitimize American intervention, either under the United Nations or by a coalition of states that might respond to a formal request for assistance. The Dulles speech and news reports of the Ely visit encouraged the Conservative opposition in the Canadian Parliament to press Pearson for an expression of Canadian solidarity with the notion of "united action," especially if, as they contended, the Chinese

were actively intervening on behalf of the Vietminh. They asked
Pearson to initiate talks for a Pacific Pact, an idea that Howard Green,
the Conservative member from Vancouver, had long favoured. Pearson
went as far as to agree that there was "real danger in the extension at
the present time of communist aggression in Indochina," but he
refused to commit the government to any specific line of action.[14] He
was sufficiently worried by reports of American thinking, however, to
ask Ambassador Heeney in Washington to obtain clarification from
Dulles.

Dulles confirmed that the United States was engaged in an effort to
form a regional coalition "on the NATO pattern" to include France, the
United Kingdom, Australia, and New Zealand, as well as Thailand and
the Philippines, in order to prevent "the further over-running of S.E.
Asia by communism." The main danger was a political, not military,
collapse in France and Vietnam, leading to a "peace at any price"
approach at Geneva. A coalition of this kind would also facilitate a
request to Congress, he said, to "grant discretional authority to the
President to use military force in support of the French effort." If the
Chinese should openly intervene, "we would expect to take such
measures as knocking out Chinese air bases ... and probably the
stepping up of activities along the South China coast," but there was
no question of bombing Peking. (It was never clear during these weeks
exactly what was meant by Chinese intervention, nor how this differed
from what the United States was already doing. The French, of course,
had a vested interest in sounding this alarm.) Dulles noted that the
French had recently asked for American assistance (this was to be an
air strike, although Heeney's report makes no mention of it) "in terms
which would have involved our belligerency"; but the United States
would only act "as part of a collective operation" and not alone — a
condition imposed by Congress. Dulles did not ask that Canada join
the coalition, but said he would be interested in Pearson's reaction to
the idea.[15]

The reaction was muted, especially after Pearson learned that the
British had objected to the timing of the initiative, doubted the gravity
of the military situation, and were concerned about the reaction of the
Asian Commonwealth members. India was sceptical, to say the least,

about "united action." The furthest the British would go in public was to agree "to examine the possibility of a collective defence ... to assure the peace, security, and freedom of Southeast Asia and the Western Pacific."[16] Pearson reported these views to the cabinet on 14 April, emphasizing that Canada would not be invited to be a member of any security alliance, and would only take part in the Indochina phase of the Geneva conference in the unlikely event she was asked. He reflected this attitude of benevolent but distant interest in an interview with the CBC before leaving for Geneva. Unless and until the United Nations were to take a decision in regard to it, Canada had "no obligations specifically directed toward that area."[17] Dulles could not have been pleased, but he was probably not surprised.

British and American differences over the appropriate Western response to the situation in Vietnam widened before the Geneva conference convened on 26 April. Pearson had become aware in Paris, on his way to Geneva, that the French were asking for American air action to save the garrison at Dien Bien Phu from defeat.* He was to learn from Eden in Geneva that Dulles had abandoned this option as too little and too late, but had been prepared, if the British agreed to help, to give the French a written assurance that the President would ask Congress for special powers to move US ground forces into Indochina and thus "internationalise the struggle against communism in Indochina." The cabinet had rejected any British participation in such a scheme because it might provoke a wider war instead of a negotiated peace based, perhaps, on the partition of Vietnam and to be guaranteed by the Geneva powers. Pearson agreed with this assessment and told the Americans so.[18]

Eisenhower, on the other hand, reacted angrily to the British attitude, accusing them privately of "showing a woeful unawareness of the risks we run in that region." The President was himself unsure of what to do about such risks, however, and it is hard to believe that he authorized Dulles to offer ground forces, as Eden reported to Pearson.

---

* This issue became entangled with that of the use of nuclear weapons. McGeorge Bundy has looked closely at the evidence as to whether Dulles or Bidault first proposed the use of nuclear weapons and concludes that it was probably Dulles. "In talk — though never in action or in formal recommendations — Dulles was a bit of a nuclear swordsman" (Bundy, *Danger and Survival*, p. 269).

He told his advisers, including Vice-President Nixon, who was a hawk on any issue involving China, that the United States should not become involved in local engagements around the world. These would ultimately sap its strength, and might lead to a world war. He ruled out unilateral intervention in Indochina, giving the British, in effect, a veto over American policy. Yet he also believed, as did most officials in Washington, that a French defeat in Indochina would lead to the loss of all of Southeast Asia; this was the so-called domino theory that Eisenhower had articulated long before it became fashionable as a justification of US policy in the 1960s.[19] It was this assumption, and the conclusion drawn from it that, if France gave up the struggle, only a regional alliance could prevent a communist sweep, that most divided the British and Americans at Geneva. Eden, in particular, who was a co-chairman of the conference, along with Foreign Minister Molotov of the Soviet Union, regarded a ceasefire and a temporary partition of Vietnam as the best outcome that could be expected at the conference, and he feared that this would be in jeopardy if the Western powers threatened instead to intervene in the area by means of a show of strength.

Pearson's position at Geneva was that of interpreter, in this case of British and Commonwealth views to American officials. Eden and Dulles were barely on speaking terms and, although Bedell Smith, Under-Secretary to Dulles, who remained in Geneva after the departure of Dulles in early May, enjoyed everyone's respect, distrust lingered.[*] Pearson was on good terms with all the Western participants. He had dealt with Eden and Casey, the Australian Minister of External Affairs, since 1951 when they both assumed their current posts, and he had come to know Bidault at NATO meetings. Eden and Bedell Smith kept Pearson informed of their conflicting attitudes on the establishment of an Asian NATO, and while Pearson supported the British case in private, he let it be known in public at Geneva that the failure of negotiations might "necessitate further

---

[*] An eyewitness account of personal relations at Geneva is given by Evelyn Shuckburgh, Eden's private secretary in *Descent to Suez: Foreign Office Diaries, 1951-56* (London: Weidenfeld and Nicholson, 1987), pp. 172-89. He notes several instances of Pearson's strong support for Eden in his dealings with Dulles. Eden's distrust of Dulles was to deepen during the Suez crisis two years later.

collective consideration, by those who ... will feel increasingly threatened, of further ways and means to meet that threat," an obvious reference to the American proposals.[20] At the same time Pearson told St. Laurent that, while others understood that Canada was not about to assume new obligations, "we would not be able to escape the consequences" if the negotiations should fail, including "a real danger of serious division" between Britain and the United States.[21] He remained in Geneva until 20 May, concerned primarily with the Korean phase of the conference (which ended in failure), and acting in regard to Indochina as an "unobtrusive oil can," in the words of John Holmes, one of his advisers at the conference.[22] Such ministrations, one can claim on the basis of sketchy evidence, probably helped to keep the conference train on the rails and the nervous Americans from disembarking.

The Americans had reason to be nervous. By the time the conference turned to Indochina on May 8, the French garrison at Dien Bien Phu had surrendered, and opinion in France was turning ever more strongly against the war. The centre-right government of Premier Laniel survived a vote of confidence on 13 May by only two votes and began once more to seek US intervention. Dulles was pessimistic: "a French collapse seemed to be in prospect as grave as the collapse of 1940."[23] This was a highly dubious analogy that most French voters would have rejected with incredulity if he had made it openly, but it illustrates the mood in Washington at the time. In Geneva the Vietminh called for the withdrawal of foreign troops from Indochina and rejected French proposals for an armistice *in situ*.

Pearson reported to the cabinet and to the Commons on developments in late May. The former appears to have received his prediction that North Vietnam would soon be controlled by Ho Chi Minh without alarm. It agreed that a security pact for Southeast Asia would have doubtful validity if its aim was simply to prevent the spread of communism, "or if the leading Asian nations were not consulted."[24] For Ottawa and London, the leading Asian nations were India, Pakistan, and Ceylon, and perhaps Indonesia. For Washington, they were Japan, the Philippines, and Thailand. Members of Parliament received a long account of the negotiations in Geneva, but only a discreet allusion to British-American differences. A regional security pact for the area, Pearson said, should be based on certain principles: UN approval, a membership of independent states, non-military as well as military objectives, and wide support in Asia. Moreover, the treaty should be designed, on the model of NATO, to prevent aggression, not the spread of communism. As for Canada, the government was naturally concerned "with problems affecting security in the Pacific and in Asia." Peace was indivisible. But there were limits to what Canada could do. If the matter were brought to the United Nations, Canadian policy might be different, and Pearson hoped that the UN "might prove useful."[25]

The government received conflicting advice from the opposition parties, as it did on most aspects of East-West relations. The Conservatives thought that Canada should join an Asian NATO if the negotiations in train failed, while at the same time they also extolled the virtues of the Commonwealth, which was divided on the issue. The CCF put the blame for the situation on French colonial policy and American tactics, and hoped the government would do nothing to alienate India.[26] Pearson was closer to the latter view, but was careful not to be publicly critical of either American or French policy. His main concern was Western unity. Speaking a week later to a meeting of historians, he allowed himself to reflect on the basics of foreign policy. Seeking to maintain unity amongst the Western allies, especially between the United States and Britain, was "a very important principle of Canadian foreign policy." No doubt having in mind the sounds of sabre-rattling in Washington, he laid emphasis on the "special obligations" of the strongest members of the alliance "to cultivate self-denying qualities of patience, restraint, and tolerance."[27] Unity was undergoing a severe test that summer.

In Geneva the negotiations were proceeding slowly, against American and South Vietnamese opposition, towards an armistice that recognized the *de facto* division of Vietnam. French Union forces holding Hanoi and the delta region in the north were gradually giving way to the Vietminh forces of General Giap, equipped with captured and Chinese weapons. Elsewhere Vietminh guerillas were in control of much of the countryside. The French proposed a ceasefire based on the patchwork positions of opposing forces, while the Vietminh preferred territorial exchanges and regroupments that would approximate a "single line" division. Military representatives of the two sides began to meet in early June to sort out these ideas, while the conference turned to the question of how a ceasefire might be supervised.

Canada's close relations with India gave Pearson a foretaste of the political difficulties involved. He had spent many hours at the UN with Krishna Menon, India's egocentric representative and diplomatic busybody, during the Korean armistice negotiations, hours to which he applied the formula "tea and sympathy"; and Escott Reid, High Commissioner in New Delhi since 1952, was well-informed about Indian thinking. In early May Menon told Reid that both China and the Soviet Union wanted to end the fighting, and would accept supervision of a patchwork ceasefire by four neutral nations; he suggested India, Mexico, Argentina, and Sweden or Norway (Norway was a member of NATO but was often critical of US policies). He did not mention Canada nor did Reid, presumably because Canada's part in the Korean War was thought to rule out membership of a "neutral" commission.[28] Menon abandoned this proposal when he later learned that China favoured a commission that reflected the views of both sides and would not agree to a ceasefire supervised by the United Nations, the preferred American solution. This was the 50 percent principle, to be reflected in a Soviet proposal on 31 May that the commission be composed of communist Poland and Czechoslovakia, and non-communist India and Pakistan. The British rejected this version of equality and returned to the idea of neutrals. They proposed that the Colombo powers fill the role (India, Pakistan, Ceylon, Indonesia, and Burma). The issue was clear: either a commission of more or less neutral countries operating on the basis of majority rule, or a commission with equal representation from both sides and therefore without the capacity to take decisions on major issues. China and North Vietnam were not about to give up at the peace table the gains they had made on the battlefield.[29]

Attention now shifted to Paris where the government of Premier Laniel faced another vote of confidence in the National Assembly.

After a two-week debate, which turned largely on the situation in Indochina, Laniel lost his majority and on 18 June, Pierre Mendès-France, a member of the Radical Party (despite their name the Radicals were in the centre of the political spectrum), was elected Premier. Mendès-France offered a bargain to the Assembly; he would end the war in a month or submit his resignation. This daring gamble was characteristic; he had resigned from de Gaulle's government in 1945, despite a brilliant reputation, and had remained an outsider, attracting both devoted admirers and the suspicions of politicians who continued to play by the rules. These were determined by a political system that obliged the non-communist parties to enter artificial coalitions in order to keep out the Communist party, which regularly obtained the largest number of votes — 26 percent in the 1951 elections. In soliciting the support of the deputies on 10 June, Mendès-France had been both critical and defiant; he would end the ambiguity and drift of previous policy and negotiate directly with the Vietminh. If an honourable settlement proved impossible, he would send conscripts to Indochina, an act that hitherto had been thought a political death wish. He capped his declaration with the announcement that he would decline the support of the ninety-nine communist deputies in the count of his majority, and in the event he did not need them.[30] *

The election of Mendès-France was followed by a pause in the Geneva talks, which in any case had ended in failure to agree on the future of Korea. An American-sponsored attempt to involve the United Nations in Southeast Asia by sending an observer team to the border of Thailand was vetoed by the Soviet Union on 18 June. Military staff talks between the United States, Britain, France, Australia, and New Zealand to consider what might be done should fighting continue had ended in Washington on 11 June, leading Dulles to conclude that the French were likely to quit Indochina. In the circumstances, the

---

* I attended the proceedings of the National Assembly as a diplomatic observer on this occasion, and was both elated by the choice of Mendès-France and depressed by the hostility of many deputies to this charismatic figure, whom they regarded as a dupe or, worse, as unpatriotic. The same doubts were held in some circles in Washington. For my part, already disillusioned by the French political scene after only eight months in Paris, here was an opportunity for France to be rid of the past and its burdens. It was not to be. Five months later conflict broke out in Algeria.

Americans were anxious to end the conference, fearing association with a sell-out.[31] Premier Chou En-lai and Molotov, the Soviet co-chairman of the conference, were no doubt aware of this preference. Accordingly, not wanting the United States to have a free hand in Southeast Asia, and perhaps encouraged by the words of Mendès-France, they began to make concessions.

Chester Ronning, the Chinese-speaking diplomat who headed the three-man Canadian delegation after Pearson's departure, was told by Chou En-lai on 19 June that China wanted to reach a settlement and was "anxious to cement good relations with all countries of the West." But he was puzzled by apparent differences of view within the American delegation and confused by the tactics of Foreign Minister Bidault. The Americans were indeed split, and as they refused to talk to the Chinese, there was plenty of room for confusion. As for the supervision of any agreement, Ronning was also told that a commission of three countries — perhaps India, Poland, and Burma or Indonesia — would be acceptable to China, provided that "important" questions were decided unanimously.

Chinese interest in a settlement was confirmed when Mendès-France met Chou En-lai in Switzerland the week following his election. The outline of an agreement appears to have been reached at this meeting, based largely on Chinese terms: the neutralization of Laos and Cambodia, and the temporary partition of Vietnam to be followed by elections. Chou promised that the Vietminh would clarify their position on the vital questions of where to draw the line in Vietnam and the date of the elections, questions on which Mendès-France would bargain hard. The election date was important because the Vietminh were confident that the sooner elections were held the more likely they were to win them.[32] It was this prospect that led Washington finally to accept partition in the hope that elections could be delayed, perhaps indefinitely, and to press for provisions that would facilitate the free movement of refugees, effective international supervision, and the right of Laos, Cambodia, and "retained Vietnam" to maintain adequate armed forces, to import arms, and to "employ foreign advisers." Mendès-France agreed to these terms and, in return, the United States agreed to "respect" the terms of an armistice based on them, although it would not associate itself with the communist Parties to the agreement by signing them. While Dulles appreciated the "frankness and sincerity" of Mendès-France he could not formally approve "successful aggression in Southeast Asia."[33]

In a whirlwind series of meetings with the Soviet and Chinese foreign ministers before his deadline expired on 20 July Mendès-France was able to secure terms for a settlement that largely met the American (and British) conditions, and the three ceasefire agreements were signed that day in Geneva. The line of division in Vietnam was placed along the 17th parallel, representing a concession by the Vietminh who had wished it to be farther south on the basis of territory they already controlled. In an unsigned Final Declaration the conference "took note" of the agreements and set the date of elections in Vietnam for July 1956, again a concession by the North. And agreement was finally reached on the composition of the control commissions: India, Poland, and at the last moment, Canada. All in all, the settlement was a major accomplishment. No one was fully satisfied, least of all the two Vietnams, and the United States refused even to be associated with the Final Declaration. But the fighting stopped, and France was in a position to withdraw from empire without undue humiliation, and without having provoked a wider war.[34]

Ottawa learned about Canada's nomination to the commissions from a *New York Times* story published on 19 July. John Holmes, the remaining member of Canada's delegation, had left Geneva on 2 July, assuming that Canadian interests could safely be left to the office accredited to the UN there. An Ottawa press report the same day quoted Canadian officials as being sympathetic to the request, which came as "no surprise" to them. This seems unlikely. Perhaps Pearson had had wind of the possibility from Churchill and Eden, who had been in Ottawa at the end of June after a visit to Washington, but as far as the department knew of the matter, the Chinese proposal that India, Poland, and Indonesia or Burma form the commission was still extant. The Geneva office, alerted by the *Times* account, discovered that China had suggested Canada instead of Indonesia after France had proposed Belgium, and that this had come as a "complete surprise" to Britain and France. Pearson reacted quickly, authorizing a press release the next day that announced that the government would give "immediate and sympathetic consideration to any request," and this arrived on 21 July.[35]

When the cabinet met on 22 July Pearson had already spoken to the Prime Minister (who was on holiday), who agreed that the invitation be accepted if there was reason to believe that the commissions "could work effectively." By 28 July when cabinet next met, this time with the Prime Minister present, Pearson had consulted London, Washington, and Paris, and he advised formal acceptance. He did so on the grounds that the settlement appeared to be workable, would not involve enforcement obligations as in Korea, and might lead to "a permanent settlement of the Indochina problem." Moreover the allies were anxious that Canada accept — a refusal could have upset the whole fragile edifice erected in Geneva — and there was "no other Western country in a better position than Canada to work harmoniously and effectively with India." The cabinet agreed, apparently without much debate, aware that the task would be "exceedingly difficult" and would last "at least two or three years." In fact, it lasted almost twenty.[36]

Surprise or not, and unwelcome as it certainly was, there could not have been much doubt that Canada would accept the invitation. Not to do so would have upset her major allies and called in question the ceasefire agreements, although China would probably have agreed to Belgium if that became necessary. For Pearson, however, the positive reasons for taking on the task outweighed the consequences of not doing so. Since 1950 he had fought the constant American temptation to expand local conflict around the borders of China to China itself. He wondered in private if Dulles's policy was aimed at the overthrow of the Peking regime, a goal openly favoured by Washington hawks nesting in high places, such as Admiral Radford.[37] He was sceptical of the value of an Asian NATO, believing that the main threat to "free Asia" was subversion, not aggression. But he also believed that collective security arrangements, whether regional or global, were a means of exercising restraint on bellicose tendencies in Washington, and he therefore gave the Dulles plan support in principle. He also thought it vitally important that senior US officials maintain confidence in Canadian judgment, and in Canada's capacity to influence other American allies and the non-aligned Asian countries. They would be more apt to do so if Canada remained both a loyal and an independent ally, willing to question American tactics but not strategic objectives such as the containment of Sino-Soviet power. Thus Pearson told the cabinet that the Chinese probably put Canada's name forward for the commissions because they thought that "Canada was the best of a bad lot," not "dominated by the US."[38]

This also appears to have been the American view, in a different sense: Canada was preferable to others who might have been asked because Canada understood American interests better. The main American interest was the prevention of further communist control over Indochina and beyond, and for this purpose Dulles expected that the Canadian Commissioners would act as representatives of their government.[39] The first letter of instructions from Ottawa to the Canadian team, however, spoke rather of "objectivity, impartiality, and fairness." We would keep our friends informed, but "we do not intend thereby to let them direct our decisions."[40] Publicly, the government announced that Canada was embarked on "an onerous but honourable assignment." The reason was that "if ... Canada can assist in establishing security and stability in Southeast Asia, we will be serving our own country as well as the cause of peace."[41] It was an assignment that was to last a generation and demand the services of some thirteen hundred members of the armed forces and one out of three Canadian diplomats.

Had Pearson known in 1954 that the assignment would also engage his own government some years later in charges of complicity in a major American war or, on the contrary, of precipitating severe strain in Canada-US relations, he might have declined the invitation from Geneva.* But I doubt it. He knew that this would be a risky enterprise, and within six months he was already worried about Polish "obstruction" and Indian "indecision" as well as reports that the United States

---

* The charges of complicity have been made by Eayrs, *In Defence of Canada*, vol. 5, and Charles Taylor, *Snow Job: Canada, the US, and Vietnam* (Toronto: UTP, 1974), amongst others. Ross, *Canada and Vietnam*, challenges this view. My own strong impression from talking with my father in the mid-sixties is that he became increasingly unhappy with American military tactics but remained reluctant to disavow the policy of offering assistance to South Vietnam.

would try to delay or prevent the holding of elections in Vietnam.[42] Such concerns were to grow in strength. Yet the original impetus for Canadian participation prevailed, and came almost entirely from Pearson himself. No one in cabinet, except St. Laurent and possibly C.D. Howe, was in a position to challenge his advice (Abbott and Claxton, the two Ministers who were both senior to him and in posts of influence, had left the government in June). Parliament was not sitting, and the public was little interested in so obscure a place on the map of world politics. Nor were officials much wiser. None had been there, and only John Holmes, the head of the UN division in the department, was familiar with the issues. Indeed, at the embassy in Paris we were asked to obtain a detailed map of the area. But this first Canadian venture into large-scale peacekeeping was more than a leap in the dark. It was also a leap of faith on Pearson's part, faith that, building on the lessons of Korea and in the shadow of the new hydrogen bomb, ways to prevent war must go beyond the threat of preparing to wage it.

CHAPTER EIGHT

The China Puzzle:
"Don't Let Asia Split the West"

IT WAS NOT an accident that three of the main diplomatic challenges to confront Lester Pearson in the early 1950s — Korea, aid to South Asia, and Indochina — had their origins in Asia. In October 1949 a communist government took control of China, and Pearson's response to these challenges was bound to be coloured by this fact. The European political landscape, in contrast, lay deep in the snows of the Cold War, and remained so for most of the decade, despite the signing of the Austrian Peace Treaty in 1955. Pearson worked hard to improve methods of political consultation in NATO, and he contributed his diplomatic skills to finding in 1954 the formula that brought Germany into NATO, but he had little fear of a war erupting in Europe. This confidence was reinforced by impressions he derived from his first and only visit to the Soviet Union in late 1955, where he interpreted the boasting and bluster of Khrushchev as evidence more of fear than of aggressive intent. As long as NATO remained strong, while avoiding military provocation, he believed that Soviet policies would stop short of war. There was no such stable balance in the Far East, where two million members of the defeated army of Chiang Kai-shek had taken refuge on the island of Formosa, and threatened, with the support of significant elements of American opinion, to return to the mainland in force. To prevent or limit conflict around the borders of China, given Canada's close relations with the United States, became a constant objective of Pearson's diplomacy, and, as President of the United Nations General Assembly in 1952–53, he found himself in direct contact with the Chinese authorities over the terms of an armistice in Korea. These, and other issues affecting China, were to strain Canadian ties with her neighbour and to cause divisions in Canadian opinion that had no counterpart in relations with Europe. Perhaps it was also no accident that the unit in the department dealing with China was called the "American and Far Eastern Division"!

In 1955 a new crisis involving China, this time between the two rival governments, was to bring the United States perilously close to war. If China were drawn into war with the United States, would her Soviet ally be far behind? Would the war then become a global conflict, with the use of nuclear weapons? How would Canada be affected? These were the kinds of questions that lay behind the Asian crises of the 1950s, and to which Canadians were becoming newly sensitive as the realization dawned that a nuclear war would most likely be fought in North American skies.

In 1948 the Canadian government lacked anything that might have been called a Far Eastern policy, although it had diplomatic missions in China and Japan. Three years later, however, Pearson noted that "Far Eastern questions now absorb much of the attention of the Canadian Parliament and government." In an article in *Foreign Affairs* he went on to describe to an American audience the role of the Commonwealth and the purposes of the Colombo Plan.[1] He made little mention of China except to express the hope that "the present unnatural alliance between Chinese nationalism and Soviet imperialism may be broken." The reference to nationalism implied that Pearson could not quite bring himself to believe in the common assumption of a Sino-Soviet bloc, and he often made clear to Americans in these years that Canada was committed to oppose aggression in Asia, as elsewhere, and not communism as such.[2] But by the same token, he would not commit Canada to the diplomatic recognition of the Peking government after the United Nations accused it in 1951 of aggression in Korea, a charge that Canada had supported. He was also concerned that the rift between American and British policies after Britain did recognize the new government in January 1950 would poison the unity of the West on issues of war and peace: "Don't let Asia split the West" became a constant refrain.[3]

The issue of recognition did not so much split the West as paralyse it. After four NATO countries — the United Kingdom, Denmark, Norway, and the Netherlands — recognized the new regime in early 1950, there was no further movement in this direction by any NATO country until the mid-sixties, and China continued to be represented at the United Nations by the government on Formosa until 1971. The temper of American opinion, increasingly hostile to China's communist regime after American troops became engaged in the Korean War, was a major reason for Western caution. Canadian attitudes, though less given to extremes, were much influenced by this American hostility to communism in China, compounded as it was by the domestic argument about responsibility for the "loss" of China. Pearson found himself faced with the task of convincing his cabinet colleagues that recognition of the new government was worth the risks, both of alienating support for the Liberal party, especially in Catholic Quebec, and of irritating Canada-US relations. The challenge was too great. In the seven months between mid-November 1949, and mid-June 1950, he brought the cabinet to the brink of recognition five times, only to have it draw back from a final decision. The last time was 21 June, four days before the outbreak of war in Korea.[4]

Pearson was strongly in favour of recognition, according to his friend and former colleague, Hume Wrong, who spoke to him about it in mid-February 1950. He had been strengthened in this view by the arguments he had heard at the Commonwealth conference in Colombo in January, especially from the British who had already made the decision to recognize, and he told St. Laurent that he would recommend recognition "without further delay" when he returned to Canada. He had informed the House of Commons on 16 November 1949, that if an "independent" Chinese government was able to demonstrate its control of the country and appeared to be acceptable to the Chinese people, Canada would "in due course" have to recognize the facts of the situation. The statement followed a cabinet decision the same day to agree in principle to recognition, subject to further discussion of the timing. After Britain, India, Pakistan, Ceylon, and the Scandinavian countries had so acted in January 1950, the time was ripe for Canada to follow, and Pearson proposed to Cabinet in early March that Canada act. The Prime Minister, however, was reluctant to move ahead, advising that they "wait on the progress of events."[5] In May Pearson presented further arguments in favour of action — Canadian diplomats in China had no status, it was Soviet policy to isolate China, the situation at the UN was anomalous, China being represented by the previous regime and so on — and the cabinet went as far as to authorize the senior Canadian diplomat in China, Chester Ronning, to open an informal dialogue with the Chinese about the procedures of recognition. Ronning did so, but when Pearson tried again in June to move the process forward political qualms in Ottawa persisted, and by the time set for a final decision on 28 June the situation had been transformed by events in Korea.[6] It would be twenty years before a Canadian ambassador arrived in Peking.

It is uncertain, in retrospect, whether this rather inglorious outcome served to help or harm Canadian diplomacy. British ties with Peking remained fragile during the Korean War and led to suspicion in Washington, although they were later to be useful in defusing crises over Indochina and Formosa. British opinion by and large supported such ties, however, and this was not true in Canada, where a decision to recognize would have been strongly opposed by the Conservative party and the Catholic Church. Nor is it likely, given the British channel to Peking, that Canada would have been a preferred intermediary for Washington, which also had access to Indian and Swedish channels if necessary. Canada had few direct interests in China; fewer than five hundred Canadians, including some two hundred missionaries, lived there in 1950, and there was little trade. The cabinet view that there was no need for haste was understandable in the circumstances, especially as the arguments marshalled by Pearson for an early decision were too abstract and legalistic to overcome the political penalties that Ministers expected they might have to pay. They did agree in the autumn of 1950 not to oppose a UN resolution calling for a change in Chinese representation, but that was the limit of Canadian flexibility in the wake of hostilities in Korea.[7]

Chester Ronning left China in March 1951 a disappointed man. His status in Nanking, where the embassy was located, had become delicate in any case, but after the UN declared China an aggressor at the end of January Ottawa had to abandon the pretence of maintaining an official presence in China. Ronning had been an invaluable source of first-hand information and analysis on China, and with his departure Pearson was obliged to rely on British and especially Indian judgments of the situation. Reports were received from Washington in early 1951 that there were disaffected elements within the Chinese hierarchy who might be ready to cooperate with the United States to "unhook" China from its alliance with the Soviet Union. If so, in the American view, the West would be wrong to offer concessions, such as recognition, to the current leadership.[8] This was the opposite of the advice of officials in Ottawa, who agreed with Nehru and Bevin that a policy of military pressure would only help to cement Sino-Soviet ties.[9] Pearson was caught in a dilemma. Having voted at the UN to condemn China as an aggressor, he was in a poor position to urge diplomatic flexibility in Washington, although he could and did warn publicly against any attempt to overthrow the Peking government by force.[*]

The Geneva conference in the summer of 1954, at which a large Chinese delegation headed by Premier Chou En-lai was present, provided an opportunity for Pearson to reconsider the policy of non-recognition. He did, in fact, speak to Chou at the conference. Although nothing of any substance was apparently discussed, the encounter must at least have helped to humanize a relationship that had previously been conducted at long distance and in frosty language.[10] The conference was unable to agree on the terms of a political settlement, however, and the stigma of aggression remained. This could only be purged, Pearson repeated later, by evidence of Chinese cooperation "in the achievement of peaceful and honourable settlements to Far Eastern problems," in order to merit "formal recognition." The issue was now assuming metaphysical dimensions; for, in order to reach such settlements, Pearson added, the West had to accept "the fact of communist power in China."[11] Indeed, had it not

---

[*] An early example of the theme of "no use of force except in retaliation for Chinese aggression" was a speech to the Canadian Society of New York on 7 March 1952, when his dinner companion was John Foster Dulles, soon to become US Secretary of State. Dulles told Pearson that his speech reflected a "negative, defeatist" policy. Pearson Papers, vol. 65, Memo of conversation 15 March 1952.

been for Chou En-lai, agreement at Geneva on a ceasefire in Indochina could not have been found.

Six weeks after agreement was reached to stop fighting in Indochina, a new threat to peace in the region began to alarm America's allies. Soon after taking office in 1953 President Eisenhower repealed Truman's 1950 order to the 7th Fleet to prevent attacks from Formosa on the mainland of China and vice versa. Dulles had explained to Pearson that the purpose of this change was "to put the US in a legal position where, if need be, it could encourage threats or feints against China" as a means of deterring an attack on Indochina and of drawing troops away from Korea. Pearson had expressed concern that the decision could lead to the US navy actively assisting raids on the mainland, a concern that Dulles tried to minimize by assuring him there were no plans for a naval blockade.[12] Dulles believed that a policy of pressure on China would help to deepen potential differences between Moscow and Peking, and a year later he claimed that this policy was working. Whether it did or not (and one may wonder how well-informed American intelligence was on the subject), the Republicans had little choice but to follow a tough line with China, given the state of American opinion on communism and Eisenhower's need to placate his right-wing followers in Congress.[13]

In fact, there was little or no serious fighting between Chiang Kai-shek's forces on the islands of Quemoy and Matsu, a few miles off the China coast opposite Formosa, and forces on the mainland, before September 1954, when exchanges of artillery fire and Nationalist bombing raids took place on and around Quemoy (possibly provoked by the imminent signing of the South East Asia Defence Treaty between the United States and Asian allies alarmed by the situation in Indochina). The status of Formosa, which had been occupied by Japan since 1895 and restored to China after the war, remained in doubt, but no one disputed the fact that the offshore islands were Chinese territory. Eisenhower and Dulles were reluctant to commit forces to their defence, an almost impossible task in any case, and set about trying to persuade Chiang to relinquish them. To do so, they had to reassure him of their determination to protect Formosa, and on 2 December Dulles and Chiang signed a treaty of mutual defence, by the terms of which the parties agreed to cooperate should an armed attack take place "directed against the territories of either."[14] The latter were defined without specific reference to the offshore islands, however, leaving an impression of ambiguity about American policy that the President was to exploit quite deliberately in the months ahead.

After a period of calm, fighting resumed around the islands in mid-January 1955, and Eisenhower decided to move a step further towards intervention. On 24 January he requested congressional authorization "to employ the armed forces of the US, as he deems necessary, for the specific purpose of securing and protecting Formosa ... against armed attack ... [including] such related positions and territories of that area now in friendly hands." His message stipulated that such authority would be used "only in situations which are recognisable as part, or definite preliminaries to, an attack against the main position of Formosa and the Pescodores" (islands off the coast of Formosa).[15] There was no explicit commitment to defend Quemoy or Matsu, but the door was clearly open to do so if the President gave the order. Congress granted him this authority with little debate and almost no opposition, conscious of a public mood that remained deeply hostile to the "bad guys" in Peking (eleven American airmen had been sentenced to prison terms in China some weeks before).

Pearson had not been consulted by Dulles about US plans to defend the offshore islands in certain circumstances, nor did he know what those circumstances might be, except for the vague conditions set out by the President. He had been surprised by a suggestion to him by Dulles that the sentencing of the American airmen might warrant a special session of the UN General Assembly.[16] Instead, he looked to possible preventive action by the Security Council, where the United States and Britain were planning to call for a ceasefire, and to the mediatory abilities of Dag Hammarsjkold, the UN Secretary General, whom he greatly admired (Hammarsjkold had been selected for the post in 1953 following a Soviet veto of Pearson's nomination to the post). His reaction to the President's message was to welcome the prospect of a UN call for a ceasefire, which the President had proposed, and to urge both sides to abandon military means to achieve territorial claims. He hoped that a conference on "Far Eastern problems" might be convened to settle such claims.[17] He was only partially reassured to hear from Dulles shortly afterwards that US purposes were twofold: to "bolster the morale of Nationalist China" in the face of threats from Peking, and to make "abundantly clear" to Peking that the United States would fight to defend Formosa.[18] Dulles said nothing about the offshore islands, however, which Pearson believed ought to be evacuated by Chiang after a ceasefire. "It would be unutterable folly," he told Canadians in a radio broadcast, "to allow these Chinese islands which are a hundred miles from Formosa to become the scene or the occasion of a major conflict."[19]

The Commonwealth Prime Ministers, meeting in London in early February at their biennial session, now took a hand in the crisis, as they had done four years earlier over Chinese intervention in Korea. To his surprise, Pearson was asked to accompany St. Laurent to the meeting. It was not the custom for Foreign Ministers to attend these meetings, but Anthony Eden had invited him at the last moment in view of the looming confrontation in the Formosa strait, and he played his usual active part behind the scenes. This was Churchill's last appearance at such a meeting — Eden was to replace him in April — and Pearson's diary is full of references to his performance, including Churchill's proposal that the Duke of Edinburgh be given the title of "Prince of the Commonwealth."[20] This and other unpredictable interventions kept everyone on edge, but on the key issue of the need to evacuate the islands Churchill was at one with his colleagues.[21] Eden and Pearson took advantage of the presence of Nehru at the meeting to resurrect the diplomacy of "good offices" they had employed over ending the war in Korea. Eden telegraphed to Dulles that if he could give assurances that Chiang would evacuate the offshore islands, he (Eden) would try to obtain via India a pledge from Peking to respect a process of "peaceful disengagement" from the islands.[22] This tactic was designed to circumvent a stalemate in the Security Council on the issue, but it failed to persuade Dulles, who replied that evacuation was not politically feasible unless China renounced the use of force in the area. He also hinted that the United States would give military support to Chiang if the islands were attacked, which was exactly what the Prime Ministers feared. Before concluding their meeting on 8 February, they agreed to support a second message from Eden to Dulles indicating that Britain would have to disassociate itself from any US military intervention in hostilities over Quemoy or Matsu.[23]

On his return to Canada, Pearson informed the State Department that Canada would also find it difficult to give political support if the United States became involved in such hostilities. He reported pessimistically to the cabinet that the Americans appeared set on trying to destroy the Peking regime, and that, in the absence of Peking, further action by the Security Council would only increase tension.[24] Shortly afterwards, however, he gave Dulles a first-hand account of the Commonwealth meeting, and was sufficiently encouraged to recommend that the British and the Indians pass the message to Peking that the United States would prevent attacks on the mainland by Chiang's forces if an equivalent assurance were to be received from Peking.[25] Either this was a misunderstanding or Dulles changed his mind — not for the first time. A week later he told Eden that the United States could not continue to prevent Chiang from attacking military targets opposite Formosa, and he reported to Eisenhower that the Commonwealth leaders failed to understand the issues, particularly the fact that Mao was determined to "destroy a rival."[26] The Indians confirmed to Escott Reid, Canadian High Commissioner in New Delhi, that Nationalist bombing raids were continuing, and they rejected the proposal that they seek assurances from Peking. Faced with this impasse, Pearson drew back from the role of mediator and discouraged his officials from pursuing ideas they had circulated to other Commonwealth governments involving the creation of a neutral zone between Formosa and the mainland.[27]

The ambiguities of American policy were partly deliberate. If Formosa were to remain in friendly hands, it was thought, Chiang Kai-shek's forces had to maintain the hope, real or imagined, that they would one day return to the mainland. But Chiang could not be allowed to think that American power would help him to achieve this objective, which neither Eisenhower nor Dulles believed to be attainable, at least in the short term. Thus Chiang was told privately that the United States would help to defend Quemoy and Matsu if the

President concluded that the main Chinese objective was to attack Formosa, and the allies were told that no guarantee had been given. But uncertainty of this kind also affected the policy-makers themselves. After a trip to Formosa in late February, Dulles was full of foreboding. It was only a question of time before China attacked Formosa, he told the National Security Council, and there was need to prepare the American public for the possible use of atomic weapons. The American intelligence estimate, however, was that the Chinese did not have the capability to seize Formosa, nor were they likely to attack Quemoy and Matsu if they feared US retaliation. Eisenhower assured Churchill on 10 February that he would do all he could "to prevent the awful catastrophe of another major war."[28] The best-informed journalist in Washington, James Reston, had to conclude by the end of March that, while no one expected a major Chinese attack on the islands to be imminent, the administration was "split from top to bottom" on whether to defend them.[29]

It was no wonder that the British and Canadians were both confused and alarmed. Canadian anxieties centred on the prospect of a chain reaction if fighting began in the Formosa strait, spread to the mainland, and then led to Soviet and American intervention. Dulles tried to reassure the cabinet when he visited Ottawa in mid-March. The United States had no desire to "precipitate fighting." Perhaps the Chinese were only engaged in "a war of nerves." But a line had to be drawn and deterrence was the best strategy to preserve peace. Pearson repeated his view that the islands were the wrong place to draw the line. They were only part of "a cleaning up process incidental to a civil war." Formosa was a different matter. Dulles did not challenge this analysis but emphasized the problem of persuading Chiang to accept it without undermining the morale of his troops.[30] In separate talks with Dulles during his visit, Pearson warned against tabling a resolution in the Security Council that was bound to be vetoed. He inquired about the idea of a neutral strip down the centre of the Formosa strait, an idea, he said, that he was not yet prepared to make public, nor would he want it to be known as a Canadian proposal. Dulles was cool to the idea. It would obscure the main issue. But if the Chinese gave some private indication of interest "then the situation would be different."[31]

Pearson's diffident presentation of the proposal and Dulles's reaction were to ensure its rapid burial, and nothing more was heard of it.

Speaking in the House of Commons a week later, Pearson advocated direct diplomatic negotiations to deal with the conflict, but he did not specify methods or subjects, and he refused to criticize American policies directly. He was satisfied, he said, that US leaders were concerned "to avoid rather than provoke conflict." It would have been closer to the truth to observe that they were willing to risk provoking conflict in order to avoid it, and that, in his view, the risk was too high. But no great issue of principle was involved, and it was not Pearson's style to criticize publicly American foreign policy on matters of East-West relations unless there was such an issue, or unless Canadian interests were clearly at stake. Winding up the Commons debate on the subject in April, and after hearing proposals from M.J. Coldwell, the CCF leader, to which he was sympathetic (such as bringing China into the UN), Pearson repeated the assurance that Canada "would stay out of this struggle for these offshore islands," adding only that "other governments would be well advised to adopt the same policy."[32]

Aside, therefore, from urging caution on the Americans and attempting, via India, to persuade China to renounce the use of force, Canada assumed a low profile during the Formosa crisis. Pearson discouraged departmental advice that the Prime Minister write to the President, as Churchill had done, or that Canada offer compromise solutions. He recommended to cabinet that Canada not endorse an Australian proposal for an international guarantee of Formosan security in return for the evacuation of the islands. There should be no Canadian commitments outside the United Nations. He was apprehensive about the possible use of atomic weapons in the area, but doubted that this issue should receive any special attention in NATO consultations.[33] There were several reasons for this low-profile approach. Canadian military commitments to NATO and to continental defence were growing, and the diplomatic burden of the Indochina commissions was heavy. The UN channel, where Canadian diplomacy was most at home, was blocked by the absence of Peking, and the Commonwealth could offer only negative advice. Pearson was well aware that, in the end, Canada's security was bound up with that of her great neighbour, and he feared that evidence of disunity would affect the security of both. Finally, he was confident that Eisenhower, if not all of those around him, wanted peace.

This confidence was not misplaced. By the end of April the tide had turned in favour of conciliation. Eisenhower resisted pressure from Chiang to allow attacks on airfields on the mainland and, although unable to persuade Chiang to evacuate the islands, Dulles responded with cautious approval to a Chinese offer on 23 April that the issue be settled peacefully.[34] This gesture by Chou En-lai was made in Indonesia at the first conference of the newly formed group of non-aligned countries, and was no doubt meant to win their favour. China may also have been influenced by Soviet efforts to reduce tensions in Europe by agreeing to accept the terms of a peace treaty for Austria, and perhaps also by fear of the American use of atomic weapons, since China had only just begun to do atomic research. For his part, Eisenhower had been looking for a middle way between threats of force and appeasement. His Democratic opponent of 1952, Adlai Stevenson, had spoken eloquently on 11 April of the futility of risking American lives in an indefensible cause.[35] After China agreed in July to the release of American airmen still in captivity, US-China talks began in Geneva and the issue disappeared for three years behind a diplomatic smokescreen.

The easing of tension in the area prompted Pearson to promise another look at the question of recognition, one that he announced publicly in August 1955 would come soon, after consultations with other governments. Foremost among these was Australia where Richard Casey, the Foreign Minister, was as sympathetic as Pearson to the need for change but faced the same problem of convincing his colleagues that the political risk was worth taking. Pearson told Casey in September that "some kind of action before long would be necessary," although he could not be specific. The issue was not one of high priority, however, and there were always good reasons for delay: continuing hesitations amongst friendly governments such as Australia and Belgium, a forthcoming visit by St. Laurent to Washington, and continuing strong opposition to change by many Canadians, including the Conservative party. At the end of January

1956 Pearson had to admit that policy would remain the same: "rejecting on the one hand immediate diplomatic recognition but rejecting on the other hand the view that a Communist regime in Peking can never be recognized as the government of China."[36] It would not be long before the attention of officials and politicians was fixed on a new threat to the peace of the world — war in the Middle East. Pearson would continue to fret about China recognition, but during his last year in office the issue would not again come to the fore.

This "cycle of procrastination"[37] continued after Pearson left office in 1957, and was not broken until 1969. Would it have made a difference if Canada had extended recognition to China in 1950, or done so in 1956 when China's relations with the West appeared to improve? Action in early 1950 might have persuaded others to follow, but it would not have changed American policy, and this was the key factor in bringing to bear influence on China. The British example is revealing. While it enabled London to communicate directly with Peking, there is little evidence that it helped to alleviate US-China tensions or increase British influence on Chinese policy, although it was convenient that Eden could negotiate directly with Chou En-lai at the Geneva conference in 1954. In 1956 the Canadians feared that the United States might withdraw from the UN if China were admitted.[38] Justified or not, such a fear induced caution. Pearson's main concern after 1955, when sixteen new members joined the UN, was that the organization, lacking a legitimate Chinese presence, would be unable to deal with Asian security questions (the Vietnam war was to become a prime example). He deeply believed in the principle of universal membership. But principles are not always compatible with practical politics, nor indeed with one another, and the failure of this principle to be translated into Canadian policy was a failure he always regretted.

CHAPTER NINE

Seize the Day:
Suez, 1956

LESTER PEARSON COULD not have imagined on 1 January 1956, even if he had been given to such fancies, that his most famous diplomatic achievement would come that year over a dispute in the Middle East, an area about which he knew very little. True, he had been closely involved in the creation of the state of Israel in 1947–48 through his work at the United Nations, and in his childhood, he recalled, he was taught more about the geography of Palestine than about that of Canada.[1] Moreover, his UN experience had convinced him of the depth of feeling on both sides of the Palestine issue: "it was a life and death confrontation between two peoples."[2] But except for a short visit to Cairo in 1955 he had been to none of the countries of the area, including Israel. He did know the Foreign Ministers of Israel and of the principal Arab states (he especially liked Fawzi Bey of Egypt), and after Israel established a diplomatic mission in Ottawa in 1953, and Canada established similar missions in Cairo and Tel Aviv a year later, he was to become more familiar with the intractable nature of the Arab-Israeli conflict. Until 1956, however, the Middle East was not high on his agenda nor on that of the Department of External Affairs, which waited until November 1956, before creating a separate division to deal with the area.

The issue that brought the subject nearer the top of the agenda was the export of arms to the area. Raids and counter-raids across the armistice lines between Israel and her neighbours increased during 1955, leading to fruitless debate in the Security Council. The announcement in September 1955 that Egypt was to buy sophisticated arms from the Soviet bloc alarmed Western foreign offices, some of which now began to regard Colonel Nasser, the Egyptian leader who had come to power in 1954, as a threat to Western interests, including principally the unimpeded flow of oil through the Suez Canal. Pearson did not hold this opinion. Meeting with Nasser in Cairo in November 1955 on his way back to Canada from a Commonwealth conference in Singapore (a Jewish holiday prevented a parallel visit to Israel), he received an impression of "sincerity and strength." Nasser told him he would have preferred to buy arms in the West but, having been refused, had turned to the East in order to counter "the boasted military superiority of Israel." Pearson told him that Israeli requests to the United States, Britain, and Canada for arms "which would add to their present level of offensive strength" had also been refused, and that all three tried to follow "an impartial policy." Pearson had recently visited Moscow — the first NATO Foreign Minister to do so — and he took the opportunity to warn Nasser against "the historic Russian designs in the Mediterranean and the Middle East," receiving the response that these were not a serious threat. Discussion of a possible political settlement between Israel and Egypt did not give Pearson any cause for optimism that one would soon be found.[3]

Neither party to this conversation appears to have referred specifically to the sale of Canadian arms to the region. Two months earlier the cabinet had rejected a request to sell forty jet fighters to Egypt, a rejection that may well have helped to persuade Nasser to turn to the East.[4] Earlier in September, however, Pearson had approved the sale of fifteen Harvard training aircraft to Egypt, and when this became public knowledge in January 1956, questions were raised in the House of Commons, obliging him to speak in some detail about Canadian policy towards the Middle East. While Canadian arms exports to Israel and Egypt in 1954–55 amounted to a total of less than $3 million, about two-thirds of these went to Israel, mostly for spare parts for tanks and anti-aircraft guns. In this light, opposition to the sale of training aircraft to Egypt was difficult to maintain and the debate degenerated into arguments about ministerial competence and opposition intentions. In his statement on the problems of the Middle

East Pearson called for compromise on both sides; the Arabs must recognize the legitimate existence of Israel, but they were also entitled to assurances of an honourable solution to the plight of Palestinian refugees, including compensation, and of a willingness to readjust borders. In response to a question from John Diefenbaker, soon to become leader of the opposition, Pearson welcomed the idea of a United Nations force to act as a buffer between Jews and Arabs: "I think there is a great deal to be said for trying to bring that kind of police force into existence ... as a provisional measure to keep the armies apart while peace can be secured." Canada would consider any proposal for Canadian participation in such a force sympathetically, but would not itself propose UN action of this kind.[5]

The idea of a UN presence in areas of conflict was not a novel concept. Some five hundred military observers had been sent to the region in 1948–49 to supervise the armistice agreements arranged by the UN, and were still present (a smaller number had been observing the ceasefire in Kashmir since 1949). Canada had agreed to contribute five officers to this group in 1954 and to provide the Chief of Staff in the person of General E.L.M. Burns. This was hardly a major commitment, but at the time Canada still had a battalion serving with UN forces in Korea and was beginning to shoulder the burden of peacekeeping duties in Indochina. Selwyn Lloyd, the British Foreign Secretary, talked in early 1956 of doubling the size of the UN observer group, and although this did not happen at the time, in part because of Israeli objections, it was logical for Pearson and others to think in such terms ten months later when the crisis erupted.[6]

Pearson remained pessimistic about finding a political settlement to the Arab-Israeli impasse. "The best we can do," he wrote to Canada's Ambassador to Israel in March 1956, "is to hope that they don't get together in the wrong way by shooting at each other."[7] He was disturbed by reports of increasing Soviet bloc military assistance to Egypt and feared that some Israelis in high places might be tempted to provoke a conflict with Egypt before the military balance turned against Israel. The cabinet agreed to his recommendation that decisions on pending Israeli requests for weapons be deferred.[8] In April and May there was new Israeli pressure, this time supported by

Foster Dulles, the US Secretary of State, to allow the export of F-86 jet
fighters. Dulles told Pearson that the United States was reluctant to be
seen as choosing sides by engaging in an arms race with the Soviet
Union. This factor, he said, did not apply as much to American allies.
Pearson sensibly responded that it would be better to consult the
Soviets on how to avoid an arms race than to pursue one by other
means.[9] A confirmed Cold Warrior, Dulles was not convinced, and the
cabinet agreed that this request too be deferred, at least until the
Security Council had finished its current deliberations. Ministers
believed that Canadian opinion was sympathetic to Israel, but would
interpret the delivery of F-86s as a "direct contribution to a possible
explosion." After further pressure from Washington, supported by the
French who had already supplied fighters to Israel and were to supply
more without advising Dulles, and a promise by Dulles that the United
States would soon announce its own plans for other kinds of military
aid to Israel, Pearson recommended in July that half the order of
twenty-four F-86s be approved. His colleagues again preferred to
postpone a decision, and by the end of the month they had further
reason to shelve the issue. On 26 July Nasser nationalized the Suez
Canal Company. The Suez crisis had begun.[10]

Nasser made this decision in apparent retaliation against American
and British announcements the week before that they were
withdrawing offers to help finance the planned Aswan dam on the
Nile, even though Egypt had been willing to accept the terms of such
financing. The reasons for refusing the funds had to do with a growing
distrust of Nasser's policies, especially his ties with the Soviet bloc,
rather than with the dam project itself. No one appears to have
considered that Nasser might react with such boldness. The
headquarters of the Suez Canal Company were in Paris and its
nationalization triggered a storm of protest in France, where Nasser
was already regarded as a malign influence on the movement for
independence in Algeria, now in its second year of armed rebellion
against French rule. Prime Minister Guy Mollet, the leader of the
Socialist party, had been in office only six months but had seen his
authority crumble as the war in Algeria intensified. Here was a cause
— the destruction of Nasser — that would carry almost unanimous

public support. Mollet compared it to resistance to Hitler; there would be no more Munichs. He told the American Ambassador at the end of July that, unless military action were taken against Nasser, "all Western positions in the Middle East and North Africa will be lost within the next twelve months." His senior Foreign Ministry official was more precise: "France might induce Israel to go to war with Egypt" if the West took no concrete action soon.[11] Dulles could hardly claim he was not warned.

British Prime Minister Eden also reacted strongly, if less dramatically. Writing to President Eisenhower on 27 July, he pointed to the threat to Western oil supplies and to maritime traffic through the canal if Egypt alone were to control its management; if political and economic pressure on Nasser were not to achieve the objective of international management then, in the last resort, the use of force would be necessary. Military plans would be prepared.[12] He wrote in this vein to Commonwealth leaders as well, and while St. Laurent replied politely, Pearson sent a worried telegram to Norman Robertson in London hitting upon the key factor in the subsequent failure of Anglo-French strategy: lack of support in Washington.[13] From the start the President warned Eden and Mollet to exhaust all alternatives before contemplating the use of force, pointing out that otherwise public opinion in the United States would react in ways "that could very seriously affect our people's feelings towards our Western allies."[14] He urged them to organize a conference of the principal maritime powers. It was agreed in early August to do this, although both the French and British made it clear they would not abandon their preparations for military action. Canadian officials learned through military contacts in London that it would be six weeks before such action could be taken.[15]

The London conference on operation of the canal was attended by twenty-two countries, including the Soviet Union and India but not Canada (which was not a major user) and resulted in a majority agreement for the establishment of a system to guarantee use of the canal for all countries, to be supervised by an international board. Pearson reported to the cabinet at the end of August that "the situation had eased a good deal," although he doubted that Egypt, which had refused an invitation to attend the meeting, would accept the proposals.[16] He was right. Talks between a committee of users and Nasser ended in failure on 10 September, and Britain prepared to take the issue to the Security Council in order, Pearson was told in London, to "establish a firm UN basis for any further action," probably taking the form of economic pressure. Meanwhile, military preparations would continue. Pearson welcomed the prospect of UN discussion, but deplored the tactic of using military threats against Nasser, and was disturbed to hear the Foreign Secretary speak of the possibility with apparent relief that Israel might "take advantage of the situation by some aggressive move against Egypt."[17] This was Pearson's first meeting with a principal actor in the crisis, Selwyn Lloyd, and he came away from it with a greater sense of foreboding than he had felt in Ottawa.

Pearson was in Paris for most of September attending to NATO business, and I recall his growing anxiety about the effects of British and French policies on the alliance at the very time he was recommending ways to improve political consultations in NATO. Neither he nor any of his NATO colleagues knew anything of French-Israeli talks on military cooperation which began that month, and were to include the British by the end of the month.[18] They knew only that Dulles and Eden, with the reluctant consent of the French, were attempting to organize an association of the users of the canal with most of the countries represented at the London meeting. Dulles had advanced this somewhat desperate expedient as a way of postponing more drastic action, including an appeal to the UN that Dulles suspected would be used as a pretext to justify the use of force. This manoeuvre failed to convince London or Paris for long, however, and the appeal went forward on 23 September, to be taken up on 5 October. It came as a welcome development to most observers, including Pearson, who informed the cabinet in late September that the situation, while still dangerous, did not appear to be leading to the use of force, and that debate at the UN would help to "moderate the Anglo-French attitude."[19] Even the embassy in Paris, where tempers were continuing to run high, reported that "the use of force is now an extremely dim possibility." Israel too was thought to be following a policy of restraint, and to demonstrate its good faith the cabinet finally approved the sale of the twenty-four F-86 fighters to that country.

These judgements were to be proved wrong, of course, but they were shared in Washington as well, where Eden was also regarded as too experienced a diplomat to risk an enterprise that, without American support and certain to alienate the UN and the Asian members of the Commonwealth, had little chance of long-term success. Nor were the French considered capable of acting alone. No serious thought appears to have been given to possible French collusion with Israel, which at the time was closer to war with Jordan than with Egypt. Moreover, it looked in early October as though negotiations guided by Dag Hammarsjkold, the UN Secretary General, might be leading to a compromise. On 13 October the Security Council endorsed a set of six principles to govern a settlement of the canal dispute, and called for direct talks between the parties. Ottawa learned from middle-level British officials that agreement was near.[20]

Unknown to all but a few in London and Paris, however, Eden and Mollet were following a second policy track, this one towards war. Meeting in Paris on 26 September and again on 16 October, each time excluding the British Ambassador from parts of their talks, they began to consider the part that Israel might play in their plans. Selwyn Lloyd returned to Paris on 23 October, this time to meet Israeli leaders as well, and a detailed military timetable was agreed upon the next day.[21] Israeli forces crossed the canal on 29 October. Ten days earlier the State Department had told the Canadian embassy in Washington that "the explosive elements in the Suez situation had now been pretty well removed."[22]

The road to war was paved with misperceptions on both sides of the Atlantic. From the beginning the British and French made clear their determination to use force "as a last resort," but neither the United States nor Canada appear to have insisted on an explanation of what this meant, nor did they openly oppose it without qualification. On the contrary, Dulles did not rule out its use, telling French Foreign Minister Pineau and Selwyn Lloyd on 5 October that a resort to force ought not to be considered "until a genuine effort has been made to exhaust all other possibilities," and that circumstances might arise "where the only alternative would be the use of force" if this were not in violation of the UN Charter.[23] Pineau and Lloyd reiterated in this conversation their conviction that negotiations would lead nowhere; they were not prepared to wait indefinitely before turning to other means, although they did not explain how the use of force could be legally justified. Yet, given the known views of Eisenhower about the use of force in these circumstances, and whatever they understood Dulles to be saying, they could hardly have been unaware of American misgivings. But what would the United States actually do if force were used? Little thought was given to this vital question by either side.

If the Europeans either misperceived or discounted American objections to the use of force, they could have been in no doubt about the sharp differences between them over the issues at stake. Both Mollet and Eden drew on their experiences of the previous twenty years to believe that appeasement of dictators would invite further demands, and they convinced themselves that Nasser was committed to the destruction of their interests in the Middle East and North Africa, in league with the Soviet Union. Public opinion in Britain was split on ways to deal with the issue, and Eden himself gave the impression, before and during the resort to military measures, of a deeply troubled leader, compelled against his better judgment to follow the French into battle. It was the French, indeed, who set the pace, supported by a public opinion determined to prevent, after Indochina, any further blow to French prestige, this time in North Africa. Algeria was governed from Paris and it was still inconceivable for most French citizens that it should be otherwise, or that Nasser should be allowed to encourage its inhabitants to rebel. French interests ran parallel to those of Israel, apparently threatened by Nasser's rearmament program, especially in the air, and keen to gain access to the Red Sea across the Sinai desert. Both had reasons to strike soon, but both also needed British support.[24]

In Washington the stakes were viewed in a much broader perspective. A Western attack on Egypt, not to speak of an Israeli attack, would turn the Arab world against the West to the profit of the Soviet Union, and it would divide the NATO alliance. Besides, it was thought, Nasser's position was weak. Economic and other pressures would suffice in time to end any threat to Western interests. In addition, the Americans still regarded the UN as an instrument of US policy (a perception that was to change later), and they feared that a Western military response to Nasser would so damage Western leadership in the Assembly as to render the UN ineffective as a deterrent to aggression by China or the Soviet Union.*

The State Department began to receive reports of Israeli mobilization on 25 October, but was unsure whether the attack would be directed at Egypt or Jordan, since there had been escalating skirmishes along the border with Jordan. An alarmed President Eisenhower issued a statement on 28 October warning Israel against any "forcible initiative," but by the next day Dulles had evidence of Israeli plans to attack Egypt "with probable participation by the French and British." The French professed official ignorance of Israeli intentions, but Selwyn Lloyd appears to have deliberately misled Dulles, telling the US Ambassador on the day of Israel's invasion of Egypt that the attack was "more likely to be directed against Jordan," and that he had "no reason to believe" that the French "were stimulating such an Israeli venture." The Israeli Ambassador told the State Department that mobilization was "purely precautionary and protective." Eisenhower and Dulles therefore had good reason to be angry when they learned of the invasion (they had been double-crossed, the President said), and they began to consider whether and how they might come to Egypt's help. They decided, as a first step, to request an urgent meeting of the Security Council, and invited the British to join them. Eden refused, and the President telegraphed to him indignantly on 30 October asking, in effect, "what is going on here?"[25] He was soon to know, for later that day he received messages from Eden and Mollet defending the declaration they had just issued that called for the withdrawal of Egyptian and Israeli forces on both sides of the canal, and which required Egypt to accept the "temporary occupation" of key points on the canal by Anglo-French forces. Both

---

* Eisenhower's relatively benign view of Nasser stands in striking contrast to the perception of Saddam Hussein, also an Arab nationalist, held by Washington in 1990, in its turn strongly reminiscent of Eden's attitude towards Nasser in 1956, including the analogy with Hitler. By 1990 the United States no longer had any reason to fear the growth of Soviet influence in the Middle East, and was more dependent on oil from the region.

governments were asked to reply within twelve hours, or face intervention by such forces "in whatever strength may be necessary to secure compliance."[26] It did not help that Eisenhower first learned of this ultimatum from a press account of Eden's speech to the House of Commons earlier that day.

Pearson heard the news of the ultimatum from Norman Robertson in London, who telephoned him that morning; others in Ottawa, including St. Laurent, learned about it from the press. When a message arrived from Eden shortly afterwards asking for Canada's support for the Anglo-French effort "to ensure the safety of the Suez Canal," there was little disposition in the East Block to respond warmly. The senior Canadian official involved at the time, John Holmes, has described the mood as "stunned and uncomprehending," although Pearson "kept cool."[27] Pearson instructed Robertson to express Canada's "bewilderment and dismay" at action taken without authorization by the UN and without consultation with friends and allies. "There is nothing but pessimism around here," he informed Robertson.[28]

In New York, Britain and France vetoed an American resolution before the Security Council calling for Israeli withdrawal from the Sinai, and the issue was then referred to an emergency session of the General Assembly. Pearson told the cabinet the next day that Canada would be in a difficult position at the Assembly, given the British-American split. Dulles had asked him to do what he could "to repair the damage."[29] Such advice was hardly necessary. Pearson had been preaching NATO solidarity for seven years, especially the vital importance of transatlantic unity. He was also mindful of the dangers to Commonwealth cooperation. India had issued a statement condemning the ultimatum, while Australia and New Zealand were siding with the mother country. The UN also faced a crisis, for the Suez affair followed by five days the entry of Soviet troops into Hungary to suppress a popular revolt against communist rule, an act that the UN could do almost nothing about in the face of Soviet intransigence.

These three concerns figured prominently in St. Laurent's reply to Eden, which the cabinet approved on 31 October. The reply was couched in terms of regret rather than anger, but left no doubt of the scepticism that governed official Canadian reaction to Eden's defence of British policy.[30] Pearson reported to the cabinet before leaving for New York on 1 November that he would try to postpone or amend any resolution unduly critical of Britain and France, and work towards a solution that would involve, as an interim step, "the provision of substantial police forces stationed on the Arab-Israeli borders to keep peace," to be followed by a conference on a Middle-East settlement. He knew through Robertson that Eden would tell Parliament later that day that he would welcome a UN force in the area.[31]

Pearson arrived in New York shortly after the Assembly convened at 5:00 p.m. He faced a chaotic situation. Egypt had rejected the ultimatum; it could hardly do otherwise, inasmuch as Israeli troops would have remained on Egyptian territory and British and French planes were bombing targets near the canal. Anticipating that the Afro-Asian members would take the initiative to produce a strongly-worded resolution recommending UN intervention to stop aggression (a procedure adopted in 1950, ironically at US initiative, in order to circumvent future Soviet vetoes in the Security Council), Dulles had moved first to introduce a relatively mild resolution that called upon "all parties now involved in hostilities" to cease fire, and on Israel and Egypt to observe the armistice agreements of 1948–49. He insisted on a vote that night, although Pearson told him before the vote that he would have preferred more time in order to consult others about amending the US draft to include provisions for a peace conference and a UN police force. Such provisions, he told Dulles, would also help Britain and France accept a ceasefire "without losing too much face."[32] It was too late and too risky, however, to try to amend the resolution that night, and after it was approved in the early hours of 2 November by a large majority (sixty-four votes to five, with six abstentions, including Canada), Pearson explained to the Assembly why Canada had abstained. He regretted in particular that there was no provision in the resolution "authorizing the Secretary General to begin to make arrangements ... for a UN force large enough to keep these borders at peace while a political settlement is being worked out." He had earlier in the evening spoken to St. Laurent and was able to announce that his government "would be glad to recommend Canadian participation in such a UN force." Knowing that Eden might be looking for a way out of the crisis, he also implied that such provisions might have elicited a favourable response from the parties, if there had been time to consult them.[33] Speaking after Pearson, Dulles welcomed this approach and hoped that Canada would make concrete proposals.

Pearson put his ideas for a UN force to Hammarsjkold later that morning (no one had much sleep that weekend), before returning to Ottawa to obtain cabinet approval. The Secretary General was sceptical, believing that Israel would refuse to accept a larger UN presence in the region.[34] He feared as well that the Assembly would interpret the idea as a way for the British and French to retire honourably from the scene, using the UN force as a cover, and would reject it for that reason. In Washington that day, the Canadian Ambassador, Arnold Heeney, on instructions from Pearson, made no bones about this objective in speaking to Dulles, who had returned to consult the President: it was "to help get the British and French off the hook," and "to restore as quickly as possible the US/UK alignment."[35] Pearson suggested that the objective might best be accomplished by a resolution authorizing both a police force and the convening of a conference, or alternatively the appointment of a negotiating committee, to work out a political settlement for the Middle East.[36] (The American account of this meeting implies that the conference would establish the police force as well as deal with the political settlement, probably reflecting some confusion in Heeney's mind, or in that of the note-taker, between the immediate need to constitute an interim force and the longer-term objective of establishing a settlement to be policed by a UN force. Pearson himself may not have been clear about this in his telephoned instructions to Heeney.) Like Hammarsjkold, Dulles was sceptical. Time was pressing, and he doubted that a UN force could be assembled quickly. Better to try to stop the hostilities and to return to the negotiations with Egypt on the management of the canal.[37]

Events moved rapidly on 3 November. Pearson started the day in Ottawa where the cabinet met at 10:00 a.m. The immediate problem was to find a way of limiting, if not stopping, the war, given the Anglo-French plan to land troops in the canal area within forty-eight hours. Eden telephoned to St. Laurent that morning to ask that these troops be included in the UN force, presumably as peacekeepers rather than combatants. Pearson must have known that this idea would not be acceptable in New York, but he was determined to seek a compromise formula if one could be found. Canadian opinion was divided, the Commonwealth was divided, and Atlantic unity was in jeopardy. Given the US reaction to his original proposal of a package solution — police force plus political negotiations — he put to the Cabinet a two-stage scheme for police action alone. This plan would begin with forces immediately available, including British and French forces and others in the area, and, later, a more balanced force representative of the UN. He told the cabinet there was "a good possibility" the Assembly would give "substantial support" to a UN force of this kind if it were to take the place of Anglo-French intervention.[38] But when Heeney consulted the State Department at noon he was warned that the plan would look like collusion with Eden, who had just announced that Britain and France would stop their military action if Israel and Egypt accepted a UN force and if, in the meantime, they agreed to the stationing of Anglo-French troops along the canal.[39] This was wise advice that Pearson acknowledged by reformulating his plan once again; the Assembly would establish a five-member committee that would submit within forty-eight hours "a plan for the setting up in the Middle East of an emergency international UN police force recruited from national military forces immediately available ..." The significance of this proposal, which Pearson took back with him to New York that evening, was that the onus of recommending the composition and functions of such a force would be placed on member states. Whether it would pass the test of Assembly politics was more doubtful, but Pearson knew that his Prime Minister would back whatever solution he thought best in the end.[40]

Pearson's new text had been shown to officials in London and Washington that day. Dulles was unavailable, having entered hospital for cancer surgery, but his absence for several weeks had little apparent effect on American policy, which retained its strongly anti-colonial flavour. Selwyn Lloyd gave Robertson the impression in London that the British might be able to accept a resolution along these lines, but "he would not promise there would not be any landings."[41] The State

Department was worried about the reactions of Nasser and suggested changes, of which the most important were: to substitute the Secretary General for the five-member committee, and to require the consent of "the nations concerned." The new text was handed to Pearson in New York that night.[42] After more polishing, the final text read:

> The General Assembly, bearing in mind the urgent necessity of facilitating compliance with the Resolution of 2 November, requests, as a matter of priority, the Secretary General to submit to it within forty eight hours a plan for the setting up, with the consent of the nations concerned, of an emergency international United Nations force to secure and supervise the cessation of hostilities in accordance with the terms of the above Resolution.

Again the Assembly debate lasted far into the night. Pearson introduced his resolution near midnight, after he and his advisers had consulted the delegations principally concerned to ensure that none would oppose it. None did. Fifty-seven of the seventy-six members voted in favour, and nineteen abstained, including the Soviet bloc, Britain, France, Egypt, Israel, Australia, and New Zealand. The Commonwealth remained split, but otherwise the key to success was the consent, if not the approval, of Egypt, from which the non-aligned members would take their cue. The attitude of India was also vital. India was the main sponsor of a resolution calling for immediate compliance with the earlier demand for a ceasefire, but agreed to give the Canadian resolution priority. Moreover, Nehru had helped to persuade Nasser to accept the concept of a UN force to be stationed on Egyptian territory. Canada's and Pearson's standing in New Delhi was high and it was this factor as much as any other that helped to bring into being the UN Emergency Force.[43]

The word "emergency" was important. Both Pearson and Hammarsjkold envisaged a two-stage process: first, a temporary force to supervise the ceasefire and withdrawal, and later, a second force to help maintain peace until a political settlement could be negotiated. Pearson did not rule out the use of British and French troops in the first phase, being fully aware that these were preparing to secure the canal by force at that moment, and therefore that the immediate choice was either the continuing unilateral use of force or a UN police action. He told Hammarsjkold the next day that he had acted quickly in order to "discourage or at least postpone" the Anglo-French invasion, and to help persuade the Israelis to withdraw.[44] Both men were pragmatists about means and idealists about ends. They knew, almost instinctively, that the goals of the Charter might more easily be realized, in a world of sovereign states, when governments faced a crisis of power and the choice became survival or defeat. Nasser faced that choice, and so, to a lesser degree, did Eden.

The military timetable frustrated Pearson's hopes. On 4 November Eden alerted Eisenhower and St. Laurent to the decision to proceed with the invasion that night. He welcomed the Canadian initiative, however, and once the UN force was in place, he and Mollet would be glad to hand over responsibility to it. Pearson accepted the challenge. Working with the Secretary General and the representative of Norway, they put together the concept and mandate of a force and by 5 November had obtained the agreement of the Assembly to appoint General Burns of Canada as its commander. Offers of troops came from eight countries, but in light of the new situation it was out of the question to include British or French forces. It was also agreed to exclude the other Permanent Members, although the United States provided air transport. Pearson's summary of the situation that day reflected his deepest convictions: "If we can exploit the possibilities of a UN force quickly and effectively we may not only find a way out of present difficulties and have saved the UN from a disastrous setback, but also have paved the way for UN progress in the whole field of collective security."[45]

There was less optimism in Ottawa, and the Prime Minister wasted no time in replying to Eden's message, ending on the sombre note: "I would not wish to leave you with the impression that, as seen from here, the situation appears other than tragic." This conclusion was mainly based, he wrote, on the fact that events in the Middle East "have cloaked with a smokescreen the renewed brutal international crimes of the Soviets," giving the opportunity "for comparisons resulting from what can seem to be disregard for the UN Charter." Such comparisons acted as a check on using world opinion to condemn Soviet conduct.[46] St. Laurent was referring to the use of force by Soviet troops that weekend to put down the popular revolt in Hungary, an act then under intense scrutiny at the UN and which Pearson had condemned the day before in the Assembly "as one of the greatest ... betrayals in history." St. Laurent's implication that Western criticism of Soviet behaviour might appear to some as hypocrisy was motivated in part by the silence of Nehru over events in Hungary. For India, Western colonialism was the larger evil.[47] In his speech to the Assembly Pearson turned the comparison to the advantage of the West by pointing out that Britain and France had agreed to hand over their role to a UN force; would the Soviet Union also accept UN intervention? If not, "never again will they be able to talk about colonial oppression or imperialism except in terms of the most blatant hypocrisy."[48] Despite this difference in emphasis, Pearson and St. Laurent were in fundamental agreement that the use of force to settle international disputes could not be condoned except as authorized by the Charter.

Under intense international pressure, including threats from the Soviet Union to intervene, as well as a run on the pound and a potential oil embargo, Eden persuaded the French to agree to a ceasefire on 6 November. His public explanation was that the prospect of a UN force made further military action unnecessary; indeed, he took credit for the creation of the UNEF. Pearson and Hammarsjkold redoubled their efforts to get the Force in the field. On 7 November the Assembly approved the Secretary General's report on its terms of reference — to secure compliance with the ceasefire and withdrawal provisions of Assembly resolutions without infringing Egypt's sovereignty — and created a committee of seven members, including Canada, to advise him.

In Ottawa the cabinet agreed to provide a battalion of infantry to the force, encouraged by a call from the President to St. Laurent, the day after Eisenhower's easy re-election, pledging American support for the UNEF and praising Canada's part in its birth.[49] This decision was premature, as Pearson discovered on 10 November, when

Hammarsjkold told him that Egypt might deny entry to the soldiers of countries allied to Britain and France and that Nasser objected in particular to Canadian troops because of the similarity with British uniforms. Pearson was acutely aware of the shock such an attitude would have on Canadian opinion, and of the opportunities it would create for his domestic critics, who had accused him of pro-Nasser sympathies. He appealed to Nehru to intervene in Cairo, and helped to persuade the Secretary General to insist on the principle that the composition of the force was a matter for the UN to decide. Nasser retreated, but he remained apprehensive about popular reactions to the Canadian uniforms, especially as these were to be worn by members of the Queen's Own Rifles. After some further exchanges with General Burns, a face-saving compromise was found: Canada would supply logistics and administrative personnel instead of infantry, a change that in fact made military sense as well as tacitly acknowledging that the Egyptian concerns were not unreasonable.[50] The government was able to claim that a Canadian contribution that was to reach some eight hundred persons out of four thousand by the end of 1956 was in balance with those of the other eight contributors (four from Scandinavia, two from Asia, Colombia, and Yugoslavia).

The UNEF provided the rationale for the withdrawal of French and British forces in December, and after steady UN and especially American, pressure, those of Israel in March 1957. Pearson spent much of that time in New York, attempting to reconcile Israeli views on the conditions of withdrawal with the determination of the majority of members that withdrawal be unconditional, believing that the time was ripe to set about laying the foundations for a more permanent peace. It was not to be. The UNEF stood guard until 1967 when Nasser demanded its withdrawal as a prelude to his own disastrous attempt to right the balance of power in that unhappy region.

Pearson was awarded the Nobel Prize for Peace in October 1957, on the grounds that "the Suez crisis was a victory for the UN and for the man who contributed more than anyone else to save the world at that time."[51] Save the world? He was just doing his job, he said to me at the time. Some thought it was a poor job, at that. In Parliament at the end of November, the Leader of the Opposition moved a motion regretting that the government had followed "a course of gratuitous condemnation of the action of the UK and France" and "encouraged a truculent and defiant attitude on the part of the Egyptian dictator." Editorial opinion was mixed. Pearson was especially sensitive to the charge, pursued vigorously by the *Globe and Mail* for example, that he had deserted the mother countries in their hour of need (not a sentiment shared in Quebec, however). He was a sincere anglophile, and while his experience before and during the Second War had led him to chafe at the apron strings of Dominion status and to help loosen them, he had continued to admire the British people, and to place greater confidence in Whitehall's knowledge of how the world worked than in that of Washington. He was careful during the debate in the House to avoid any direct criticism of British policy, other than to regret the lack of consultation and "the use of force in these circumstances." He was equally, if not more, critical of American tactics at the UN. In contrast, Canada had been "as helpful to the UK and France as we possibly could be."[52]*

Pearson took no special credit for having advanced the proposal for a UN police force. He told the House he had discussed the idea with the British as early as 1953, when it was then judged to be impractical, and again early in 1956. But now "we may have started something of immense value for the future ... a step to put force behind the collective will of the international community under the law." The immediate objectives were to establish conditions for the UN to work out "an enduring and honourable settlement for that area," and, just as important for Canada, to "restore unity amongst the allies."[53] Pearson, the pragmatic idealist, had joined together the principal

---

* He was less charitable in private. Writing to a friend in January 1957, he remarked: "How the British ever expected to get away with military action with the Americans strongly opposed, with the Asian members of the Commonwealth even more strongly opposed, with the certainty that the matter would be referred to the UN Assembly where the UK and France would be in the dock ... and with the knowledge that the Communists would exploit the situation to their own advantage, is something I will never know" (letter to N.A.M. MacKenzie, 17 January 1957, Pearson Papers, vol. 34). But British leaders remained grateful to Pearson. Harold Macmillan noted in his memoirs: "Both by his personal powers of negotiation and by the respect in which he was held, he was able to exercise throughout the crisis a modifying and humanising influence" (*Riding the Storm*, [London: Macmillan, 1971], vol. 2, p. 163).

imperative of Canadian foreign policy — transatlantic unity — with his own vision of a more secure world. Peace in the Middle East remained a distant prospect, but the gleam of a future world police force helping to limit conflict, if not always to prevent it, was gradually to glow more brightly after the spark was lit at Suez.

So, too, was Pearson's own future to brighten. As early as February 1956 he had remarked to me in a letter to Paris that St. Laurent's leadership was growing weaker, with resulting pressure on Pearson "to indicate that I would accept the leadership, if offered." He had given no encouragement to such feelers, but his letter also noted that the controversy in the House over the export of arms to the Middle East had given him a chance to try his hand at debating and that he had "rather enjoyed it." St. Laurent's leadership continued to falter that summer, while Pearson's performance later at the UN was to win him new support at home as well as abroad. He did not actively seek the leadership, but when the challenge arrived in 1957 he was ready for it, and the award of the Nobel Prize removed any doubt that he would meet it successfully. He was to find that leading a political party was a much more gruelling test of character than the diplomatic round. But that is another story.

CHAPTER TEN

A Pearsonian Consensus?

REFLECTING ON THE Suez crisis in one of his last speeches before the election of June 1957, when the Liberals lost office after twenty-two years in power, Lester Pearson defined Canada's greatest interest as "international peace and security," and he added: "This interest is prejudiced when there is division within the Commonwealth or between London, Washington, or Paris." It followed, therefore, that Canada must do what she could to promote Atlantic unity, especially between the United States and Britain. Besides, it was "a first principle of Canadian foreign policy to cooperate closely with the two countries with whom every impulse of sentiment, history, self-interest, trade, and geography counsels such cooperation." When they disagreed, "we are in trouble."[1] In a subsequent interview with *Maclean's* magazine, Pearson agreed that this dilemma might be described as a kind of schizophrenia, and that in such circumstances "we instinctively try to find some kind of solution on which the British and Americans can agree."[2] In 1956 the result of this schizophrenia was the United Nations Emergency Force.

There was a text and a sub-text in this chain of reasoning. The text was the over-riding need to prevent war "in this thermonuclear age" (a favourite phrase of Pearson's) by all means available, of which the principal in the short term was the maintenance of a balance of military power. This, in turn, depended on Western unity, in particular between the United States and Britain, the two strongest NATO members. The sub-text was the natural Canadian propensity to promote such unity for the reasons Pearson gave. There was also an additional reason. Senior Canadian officials had observed the failure of appeasement to prevent war in Europe in 1939, and then watched in frustration as the United States did little to help Britain and the dominions resist the tide of German conquest until the attack on Pearl Harbor in December 1941. They were determined to keep the United States engaged in a system of collective security once it became clear to them by 1948 (rightly or wrongly) that the history of the 1930s might be repeated. It could be assumed, therefore, that the interests of Canada, however narrowly defined, were identical most of the time with the collective interests of the West as a whole. Pearson sometimes extended this concept to the whole of humanity. "In formulating a foreign policy," he wrote six weeks before he died in December 1972, the question of the Canadian future should never be separated from a wider question: "What kind of world do we want?"[3]

There was a third, if less explicit, moral that Pearson drew from his experience. This was the part to be played by Canadian diplomats in world affairs, above all by Pearson himself. "Canada's Place in the Sun" was the heading given by one magazine to a Pearson article on foreign policy in 1950, a heading that he himself did not provide but which perfectly reflected the search for recognition of a "distinct" country that occupied the diplomats of the East Block at the time. Far from waiting on London or Washington for guidance, these officials hoped to break new ground, secure in the knowledge that public support and the promise of the Canadian future would allow them to shape their own agenda of collective security, Commonwealth cooperation, and freer trade in the mould of a new Canadian nationalism.

Foreign policy is not a science. There was no Einstein in an Ottawa backroom trying to piece together the laws of collective security. The concept is as old as human society, but it was given new meaning after the failure of the League of Nations to preserve the peace, and the lesson drawn in 1945 that the United Nations must be given the means to do so. Canadians contributed only modestly to the drafting of the UN Charter, but they were amongst the first to offer military assistance to the Security Council, and in the forefront of early UN efforts to mediate disputes in post-colonial Asia and in the Middle

East. It was in Europe, however, that the organization of collective security mattered most, and there it broke down in acrimony and fear over the future of Germany and the meaning of political freedom in the states bordering the Soviet Union. Soviet hostility to a European settlement on terms the West could accept came reluctantly to be acknowledged in Ottawa, where officials began to examine alternatives to a UN system of collective security, including regional alliances or, as St. Laurent proposed in 1948, a "collective security league" made up of some or all "free states." A return to the anarchy of great power rivalries, this time under the shadow of the atomic bomb, was unthinkable.

The British and Canadians shared the view that any new system of security must be more than a military alliance if the United States were to be fully committed to the defence of the free world. They perceived a double threat — communist subversion as well as Soviet hostility — and accordingly the need to create a "dynamic counter-attraction to communism."[4] This was the goal of an Atlantic community. It was especially suited to the Canadian situation, for both domestic and external reasons. Moral idealism came naturally to Pearson and Reid, but it was also congenial to St. Laurent, more aware of Quebec's preference to fight religious wars than to appear to be defending the Empire. Nor was Canada likely to be distracted, as the British were, by the rival concept of European union, or by the American temptation to find safety in atomic isolation. Moreover, Atlantic visions provided Canadian officials with opportunities to exercise the kind of leadership that eluded them during the war and immediately afterwards. When the NATO treaty was signed on 4 April 1949, it was Pearson among the eleven Foreign Ministers present who most looked forward to the creation of an Atlantic community.

It was the United Nations, however, that continued to be the preferred Canadian instrument for the practice of collective security, if only because a UN that worked the way the Charter prescribed would reflect cooperation, not conflict, between the two great powers, and offer a forum for Canadian diplomacy that maximized Canadian status in the hierarchy of nations and enhanced its growing reputation for objectivity amongst new and old states alike. If and when the Security

Council were to function as intended, NATO, it was thought, would cease to be necessary, an expectation that was reflected in the treaty's provision for review after ten years, which Canada strongly favoured.[5] But the Cold War only intensified during Pearson's tenure as Minister, despite an occasional thaw, and he came to hope that NATO might serve a purpose that he had not foreseen in 1949: the restraint of American belligerence in East Asia, as well as of Soviet power in Europe.

The method of constraint that Pearson advocated was political consultation in the NATO Council, a method that implied both a willingness by the stronger allies to take account of the views of the majority, if these coincided, and a readiness by the others to risk the accusation of ignorance or naïveté, or, worse, disloyalty (could they be trusted with confidential information?). Pearson's attempts to make NATO work as a kind of ideal family were based in part on his own excellent relations with most of his fellow Ministers, but as they only met for two or three days twice a year they could do little more than housekeep. American policies outside Europe, or the concerting of views on colonial issues at the UN, were usually the subject of bilateral rather than multilateral diplomacy. The British had more influence in Washington than anyone else, and Pearson looked to London as the key to Atlantic unity. The British failure to consult their allies over Suez represented both a personal sense of betrayal and the failure of his efforts to strengthen such unity. It was Europe that moved towards union after 1956 and would exert the greater pull on British policy as the years passed. But if consensus on how to build an Atlantic community could not be reached, Pearson never abandoned the goal. Ten years later he spoke of a united Europe "as a stage on the way to Atlantic union."[6] If he had lived to see the end of the Cold War, however, he would have been less concerned about the future of NATO than about how to make the UN work as he had hoped it would in 1945.

The Cold War determined the limits of Canada's place in the sun during this period. In North America Canada's strategic situation on the polar route between the two great adversaries implied a continental approach to defence policy, and, given the strength of anti-

Soviet opinion in the country, there was little opposition to such an approach, provided the appearance of Canadian sovereignty was observed. NATO solidarity in the face of Soviet military power and communist subversion, and the commitment of Canadian forces in 1951 to the defence of Europe, placed a further limit on Canadian independence of action. After the outbreak of war in Korea, however, and the impetus this gave to the rapid build-up of American arms, Pearson began to fear that American policies might lead to war with China and then to a third world war. The UN response to aggression in Korea would help to prevent such a catastrophe, he believed, as long as it was limited to the defeat of aggression and did not extend to an attempt to conquer communism "as a society" or "as an idea."[7] But how was aggression to be defined, and how ended? Who would decide how and when to fight under the banner of "collective security"? How much force was enough? These were questions not easily answered, then or later.

The Korean experience led to soul-searching in the Department of External Affairs. Canada had earmarked the brigade sent to Korea for use in carrying out Canadian obligations "under the UN Charter or the North Atlantic Pact," and by this was meant an obligation to resist aggression if the UN so decided.[8] Pearson hoped that if enough UN members earmarked national contingents for this purpose the UN would be able to deal with aggression promptly, without having to rely on "one or two alone." It would be the test of "this new effort to put force behind the collective will for peace of the UN."[9] He went further. There would be advantages in the creation of "one or two genuinely UN police Divisions" composed of individuals to be trained by the UN. He hoped this idea would be studied.[10] A year later his approach was more cautious. Only eleven countries had earmarked contingents, and the idea of a "UN legion" had been met with scepticism. His officials doubted the UN's capacity to direct military operations, preferring the NATO model, and he allowed himself to be persuaded that "unlimited collective action everywhere might mean in practice no real security anywhere." Only in some regions could aggression be countered "with every military resource," and this could best be done by regional security pacts such as NATO.[11] Thus by the end of 1951 idealism had come to terms with realism. The Cold War took priority again.

If the Korean example was only a poor copy of the Charter blueprint for collective security, and if the UN's capacity to use force was to continue to be paralyzed by the Cold War and atomic stalemate, might there nevertheless be circumstances where the UN could act to prevent war, or to help restore peaceful conditions? The obvious place was the Middle East, where conflict was both endemic and outside the immediate spheres of interest of the super powers, although France and Britain continued to look upon the area with paternal concern. After these conditions led to the creation of UNEF in 1956, Pearson described the new instrument as halfway "between the passing of Resolutions and the fighting of a war." It was "a new concept of UN supervisory action," but it required the same preparatory steps by government that he had urged in 1950: the earmarking of national contingents in advance, this time "for the more limited duty of securing a ceasefire already agreed upon."[12] It could not be deployed without the consent of the governments concerned (Israel refused to allow UNEF on its soil), and it would not fight except in self-defence. The model functioned in the Middle East, and again in the Congo and in Cyprus in the 1960s, but, except for Canada, Austria, and the Scandinavians, UN members remained reluctant to commit forces in advance of operations, even though such commitments would not imply actual use without their agreement. Nor did successive Secretaries General, lacking the support of the Soviet Union and with little encouragement from the other Permanent Members or from the non-aligned majority in the Assembly, feel strong enough to take a lead. (The situation remained this way until June 1992, when Secretary General Boutros-Ghali, newly in office, and taking advantage of the Soviet demise, recommended the earmarking of military units for both peacekeeping and enforcement).[13]

Pearson's principal diplomatic objective was always to ward off the threat of a third world war by mixing power and diplomacy. In doing so, he aimed to build institutions, whether regional (NATO) or universal (the UN), which would help to nurture friendly relations amongst states and peoples, and lead gradually to some form of unity amongst some or all of them. He accepted the concept of military deterrence — prepare for war if you wish peace — not only because there was no realistic alternative to Cold War rivalry, if not conflict, but also because he believed that the accumulation of preponderant force, disciplined by collective agreement, would alone serve to deter or limit its use by aggressor states. The prospect of the use of nuclear weapons both enhanced the importance of this objective and modified the tactics he thought necessary to achieve it. Would the potential use of tactical atomic weapons deter local conflict, and if not, would their use increase the risk of general war? He had no clear answers to these questions. Neither did others responsible for the security of their countries, although the pundits delighted in the elaboration of theories of nuclear deterrence that seemed to justify the use of such weapons in certain circumstances. But such questions raised doubts in his mind about the threat or use of force by the United States, except in self-defence, even under the guise of collective security as represented by UN action in Korea. Sino-American relations provided the principal occasion for such fears, and the risks of war with China came to dominate Pearson's relations with Acheson and Dulles, as well as to underline the challenges and dilemmas of reconciling the precepts of liberal internationalism with the tough realities of Canada-US relations.

At one of his last interviews as the Secretary of State for External Affairs, Pearson was pressed hard by his journalist friend and admirer, Blair Fraser, to explain why Canada had still not recognized the government of communist China — was it mainly to avoid a fight with "certain American senators and voters"? Pearson admitted that this was a factor but, obviously uncomfortable with the subject, went on to say that it was not a matter of major principle or of vital interest to Canada, and that on such matters Canada would not hesitate to go against American opinion or policy; he pointed to the issue of the offshore islands where Canada had opposed the use of force. He noted also that Canadians were divided on China policy.[14] He might have added, in the words of one perceptive student of his diplomacy, that he was "allergic to empty, futile or otherwise counter-productive gestures," and well understood that on most major issues it was the lot of smaller states "to play upon the margins of the international political process."[15] He was fond of a cartoon that showed a family en route by car for a vacation; mother turns to the children in the back seat with the admonition: "Don't bother daddy when he is passing on a curve." If and when the United States was engaged in apparently dangerous diplomatic behaviour, would a Canadian intervention increase or lessen the danger? Would a decision to recognize China in 1954–55 have done other than raise the political temperature in Washington, not to speak of Ottawa where the Conservative opposition would have reacted angrily? And what difference would it have made to Canada's relations with China, or to China's relations with other countries? On the other hand, there were times when back seat driving might be justified. British and Canadian warnings against the use of American military power to deter or punish China in 1954–55 may have helped Eisenhower to ward off Pentagon pressure to bomb China with atomic weapons. In such cases, the "margins of the international political process" can provide a point of leverage.

Such warnings could be conveyed privately at meetings of the NATO Council or directly to the State Department, or in public speeches. Pearson resorted to both methods. He took advantage of the many invitations he received to speak in the United States to build up his reputation as a genuine but not uncritical friend, and to impress upon his audiences the value of allies and the duties of leadership. In private, he defended the British, and especially the Indians, against charges of double-dealing, sometimes incurring American suspicions that he was not above such practices himself (Acheson implied as much).[16] Loyalty was legally enforced on American officials, and, by extension, was expected of American allies. But loyalty to what? In the early 1950s a majority of Americans believed that the United States should use atomic weapons if war began with China.[17] So did senior officials in Washington. In the hothouse Washington atmosphere of the Republican 1950s it was even more difficult to be a "liberal," whether of the domestic or the foreign variety, than it was in the 1980s.

In Canada, however, diplomats were still preferred to warriors. The Liberal party dominated the political landscape, winning 190 seats in 1949 and 171 seats in 1953. Until the Suez affair in 1956 the

Conservatives could find little to criticize in Liberal foreign policy, and the CCF, although uncomfortable with the bonds of alliance and the rhetoric of the Cold War, generally supported it. Most of the journalists who wrote on public policy relished their role as interpreters of Canada's part in the new internationalism to a Canadian public hungry for self-esteem, and largely dependent on American, British, and French correspondents for foreign news. Pearson excelled at briefing the Ottawa press corps, many of whom were friends, and he kept in close touch with the editors of the major papers, especially the influential *Winnipeg Free Press* and the *Montreal Star*. Quebec opinion remained relatively quiescent, and its few isolationist voices had little effect on the majority view that communist governments were the handiwork of the devil.

Pearson could rely on St. Laurent to explain and defend Liberal foreign policy to his francophone compatriots, and indeed to all Canadians. St. Laurent's fireside chat manner gave everyone confidence that Canada was in good hands. The relations between the two men went far to create and sustain this consensus. Until Suez, the Prime Minister's judgment on the domestic implications of foreign policy decisions was sure. Once he determined what these were, as in the case of China recognition, he was content to let Pearson operate without interference. Unlike Churchill's relations with Eden, there was no competition for diplomatic stardom or the favours of Washington. St. Laurent had no need to be jealous, nor did he play favourites. After Abbott and Claxton left the cabinet in 1954 competition for the succession was muted. Pearson was not at all sure that he wanted it, despite the urgings of some of his friends. His heart belonged to global, not national, politics.

This virtual unity of minds in Ottawa, and a "let Mike do it" attitude in the rest of the country (at least until the controversy over Suez, and even then there was pride in the creation of UNEF), has been labelled "Pearsonian." The label denotes rather a style and a habit of mind than the substance of policy. Canadians were caught in the dynamics of the Cold War and the consequent strategic alliance with the United States as embodied in NATO and in continental defence cooperation. They looked to UN diplomacy and to the link with the

Indian sub-continent through the Commonwealth as vehicles for the expression of Canadian ideals. The concept of collective security had won wide approval, although its meaning was never clear-cut. Pearson added to this basic consensus a sureness of diplomatic touch and a rational approach to politics that sometimes hid the moral vision of a world without war, but which, combined with this vision, gave confidence to Canadians that Canada had a place of honour among nations.

Yet, if there was consensus in Canada, it did not always include Canada's allies. Pearson's goal of an Atlantic community was shared by only a few of his diplomatic colleagues, such as Halvard Lange of Norway and, most of the time, by the Dutch and the Belgians. After initial enthusiasm, the British preferred to emphasize their "special relationship" with Uncle Sam and their shrinking but still global responsibilities. The French had to grapple with the military burdens of North Africa and Indochina, and the Americans with the problems of leading the free world. American leaders were much readier than Pearson to threaten the use of force against communist foes, and the British and French to use it against the enemies of empire. Military pressure, not conciliation via New Delhi or Stockholm, was the preferred means of changing minds. But when it came time for final decisions, neither Truman nor Eisenhower were ready to use atomic weapons, and on that question a Pearsonian consensus held.

It applied as well to the development of UN peacekeeping. Pearson regarded human conflict as the norm, not the exception. That being so, it had to be regulated and limited by law and convention, with the Charter as a guide. But he was not a fundamentalist. The spirit of the Charter, not the letter, was what mattered, and if the Security Council failed to stop or respond to aggression, then the Assembly ought to be able to act if the situation allowed it. Clearly, action against a great power would be impractical, but in the circumstances of November 1956, the opportunity presented itself for Assembly action with the consent of the powers involved, and thus for progress towards Pearson's goal of a functioning UN police force. Consent was crucial. Without it, the UN could not have saved Egypt or the world from a wider war. Helping to obtain that consent, and then building on the opportunity created to put together the first military force responsible only to the UN, was a crowning achievement of the Pearsonian consensus, shared alike in Washington, London, New Delhi, Cairo, and Ottawa.

Now, with the end of the Cold War and the less obvious dominance of the United States in world affairs, there are more opportunities for a creative Canadian diplomacy than at any time in the postwar years. Government policies are subject to more critical assessment than they were, but on the whole Canadians remain attached to the ideals of liberal internationalism as exemplified by UN peacekeeping and aid to the victims of war and poverty. Two factors in particular have added force to these ideals since Pearson's time. One is the growing multicultural character of Canadian society. Ottawa has little choice but to respond as best it can to disaster and disorder in many more countries than was the case forty years ago. There is new reason, therefore, to work through, and to improve, the regional and global arrangements available for relief, especially the UN. Secondly, the concept of sovereignty is becoming ever less relevant to the well-being of large sections of humanity, despite the emergence of new states that lay claim to it. Violence and penury combine to drive millions of people to seek help outside their borders — borders that in any event are breaking down under pressure from the steady advance of both technology and education.

It is tempting in these circumstances for relatively prosperous and peaceful states, individually or in combination, to erect new barriers to the movement of peoples, and to draw military lines in the sand or wherever else their interests may be affected. Canadians are not exempt from such reactions, and Pearson would have been keenly aware of them. Yet he would also have welcomed the new opportunities for collective action that are offered by the collapse of Soviet power and the acceptance by the Security Council of a responsibility for humanitarian relief. He would have supported the UN Secretary General's appeal to member states to earmark units for peace enforcement as well as for the more traditional tasks of peacekeeping. He believed that in a world of sovereign states, the risks of using collective force are preferable either to its unilateral use or to a return to isolationism. Equally, however, he would have attached importance to the moral and political legitimacy of UN action to keep the peace, and therefore to the need to bring the composition and the powers of the Security Council into line with the new realities of world politics at the end of the century. Finally, he would not have doubted that, despite and perhaps because of the pressures for North American free trade, it continues to be a Canadian interest to enlarge the boundaries of regional cooperation, and to work towards universal arrangements for the peace and good order of the family of nations. The Canadian experience of flexible adjustment to shifting social and political conditions, he would have thought, could still be helpful to the building of an international order founded on minority rights and democratic values, provided we could muster the will and secure the leadership to preserve such rights and values at home.

NOTES

PREFACE

1.   The most notable accounts 'from the inside' are: John Holmes, *The Shaping of Peace* (2 vols., Toronto: University of Toronto Press, 1979 and 1982); Escott Reid, *Radical Mandarin* (Toronto: UTP, 1989); George Ignatieff, *The Making of a Peacemonger* (Toronto: UTP, 1985); Arnold Heeney, *The Things that Are Caesar's* (Toronto: UTP, 1972); and Charles Ritchie, *Diplomatic Passport* (Toronto: Macmillan, 1981). John English, *Shadow of Heaven* (Toronto: Lester & Orpen Dennys, 1989), and *The Wordly Years* (Toronto: Random House, 1992), has written the best account of Pearson's life 'from the outside.'

INTRODUCTION

1.   Department of External Affairs (DEA), Statements and Speeches (S/S) 47/1, 11 January 1947.
2.   Escott Reid, "The Conscience of the Diplomat," *Queen's Quarterly* (Winter 1967).
3.   G.M. Young, *Victorian England, Portrait of an Age* (London: Oxford University Press, 1953), p. 103.
4.   James M. Minifie, *Canada, Peacemaker or Powdermonkey* (Toronto: McClelland and Stewart, 1960).
5.   *Foreign Policy for Canadians* (Ottawa: Information Canada, 1970). Liberal internationalism has been described as a "constant co-operative endeavour to enhance universal values through the steady development of a more institutionalized and just international order." See D. Dewitt and J. Kirton, *Canada as a Principal Power* (Toronto: John Wiley, 1983), p. 22.

CHAPTER 1

1.   He wrote in his memoirs: "I have never known a finer gentleman, or one who had a greater sense of public duty." See *Mike: The Memoirs of L.B. Pearson* (New York: New American Library, 1973), vol. 1, p. 293.
2.   There is a dramatic account of King's suspicions in early 1948 of the approach of St. Laurent and Pearson to Canada's UN commitments in J.W. Pickersgill, *My Years with Louis St. Laurent* (Toronto: UTP, 1975), pp. 41ff.

3.   As Under-Secretary, nevertheless, he had to work with them closely. A letter to
      Norman Robertson of 22 April 1948, for example, describes his role in bringing
      to a conclusion the Canada/US free trade talks of that year. NAC, Pearson
      Papers, MG26 N1, vol. 13.
4.   Pearson, *Mike*, vol. 1, pp. 299-300.
5.   Ibid., p. 301. It is not clear whether St. Laurent had spoken to him before the
      convention about joining the cabinet. King noted in his diary for 8 March 1948
      that "Pearson had told him [St. Laurent] about conversations he had had with
      me previously about going into politics. St. Laurent would like to see him in
      public life." But on 11 August, St. Laurent was wondering to King "if he would
      be justified in trying to induce Pearson to come into the House." See J.W.
      Pickersgill and Donald Forster, *The Mackenzie King Record* (Toronto: UTP,
      1970), vol. 4, pp. 255, 267.
6.   NAC, Pearson Papers, MG26 N1, vol. 13.
7.   Paul Martin recalls that "St. Laurent presided magisterially over the cabinet, and
      displayed an extraordinary capacity to master his brief. He usually knew each
      submission as well as the Minister who was proposing it." See Paul Martin, *A
      Very Public Life* (Toronto: Deneau, 1985), vol. 2, p. 17. Ibid., p. 68. St. Laurent
      told an interviewer in 1970 that "I did not worry about the problems he
      [Pearson] had to deal with." Department of External Affairs, oral history
      project.
8.   Ignatieff, *The Making of a Peacemonger*, p. 111. See also Heeney, *The Things that
      Are Caesar's: Memoirs of a Canadian Public Servant*, p. 137. Bruce Hutchinson, a
      journalist who knew him well, also professed to detect "a deep gulf of
      reticence" (*The Far Side of the Street* [Toronto: Macmillan, 1976], p. 249).
9.   One of the best students of Pearson's diplomacy has remarked that he "tried to
      minimize the impact of 'non-negotiable' influences on the conduct of
      diplomacy, and believed that in politics the moral calibre of decisions could be
      tested only by reference to their results." See Denis Stairs, "Present in
      Moderation: LBP and the Craft of Diplomacy," *International Journal* (Winter
      1973-74).
10.   L. B. Pearson, *Words and Occasions* (Toronto: UTP, 1970), p. 14.
11.   Pearson's speeches from 1944 to 1947 set out hopes for collective security that
      had to be modified in practice when war with China appeared to be a
      consequence of the Korean operation. For a rigorous analysis of the dilemma,
      see Peter Gellman, "Lester B. Pearson, Canadian Foreign Policy, and the Quest
      for World Order" (Ph.D. thesis, University of Virginia, 1987).
12.   DEA, S/S 47/10, 17 May 1947.
13.   "On Human Survival," *Saturday Review*, 13 June 1970, p. 14.
14.   Holmes, *The Shaping of Peace*, vol. 1, p. 297.
15.   Pearson, *Mike*, vol. 2, p. 289.
16.   Arthur Schlesinger, Jr., *New York Review of Books*, 16 February 1989.
17.   J.L. Granatstein, Robertson's biographer, traces this tension to 1941, when
      Robertson was appointed to the senior position in the department. It was

certainly not evident in the relations between the families. See *A Man of Influence*, (Toronto: Deneau, 1981), pp. 251-52. An appraisal of Robertson by a close colleague is in Hugh Keenleyside, *Memoirs*, vol. 2 (McClelland and Stewart, 1982), p. 119-25.

18. "It was a joy to be from 1946 to 1952 a member of a brilliant team of officers in the Canadian foreign service at home and abroad" (Reid, *Radical Mandarin*, p. 242). He noted with pride that one out of eight of his then colleagues had written books, failing to mention, however, that he had written more than any of the others!

19. See the review of Reid's memoirs by James Eayrs in the *Dalhousie Review* (Summer 1989), p. 276.

20. J.L. Granatstein, *The Ottawa Men* (Toronto: Oxford University Press, 1982), p. 237.

21. NAC, Heeney Papers, MG30 E144, vol. 1, 16 February 1949.

22. Report of the Department of External Affairs, 1948.

23. Marcel Cadieux, *Le Ministère des Affaires Extérieures* (Montréal: Éditions Varietés, 1949), pp. 91 and 96.

24. Ritchie, *Diplomatic Passport*, p. 44.

25. Dean Rusk, *As I Saw It* (New York: Norton, 1990), p. 527.

CHAPTER 2

1. Quoted in Dean Acheson, *Present at the Creation* (New York: Norton, 1969), p. 222.

2. George Kennan, *Memoirs 1925-1950* (New York: Bantam Books, 1969), p. 378.

3. Joseph S. Nye Jr., *Bound to Lead: The Changing Nature of American Power* (New York: Basic Books, 1990), pp. 74-76.

4. Quoted in Alan Bullock, *Ernest Bevin* (New York: Norton, 1983), p. 350.

5. Arnold Toynbee, *Survey of International Affairs, 1947-48* (London: Oxford University Press, 1952), Introduction, p. 8.

6. NAC, King Papers, vol. 433, Wilgress to SSEA, 25 April 1947.

7. Quoted in Page and Munton, "Canadian Images of the Cold War, 1946-7," *International Journal* (Summer 1977), p. 529. Escott Reid, *Time of Fear and Hope* (Toronto: McClelland and Stewart, 1977), p. 31.

8. House of Commons, *Debates*, 4 July 1947, vol. 6, p. 5078.
Cited in DEA, *Annual Report, 1948*, p. 17.

9. DEA, *Documents on Canadian External Relations*, 1946, vol. 12, p. 1671.

10. Ibid.

11. DEA, S/S 47/16, 7 October 1947, p. 15.

12. Pearson, *Words and Occasions*, pp. 67ff. The quotes from Stalin in this speech were often used by Western spokesmen at the time and were repeated in Pearson's maiden speech to the House of Commons on 4 February 1949.

13. Cited in "External Affairs," the department's monthly journal, July 1948, p. 7.

14. Pearson Papers, address at Rochester University, 16 June 1947.

15. Holmes, *The Shaping of Peace*, vol. 2, p. 69.
16. Pearson to Toronto Board of Trade, 26 January 1948, S/S 48/2.
17. DEA, *Annual Report, 1948*, p. 18. S/S 48/2.
18. House of Commons, *Debates*, 1948, vol. 4, pp. 3438ff.
19. Pearson, *Mike*, vol. 2, p. 128.
20. Pickersgill and Forster, *Mackenzie*, vol. 4, p. 155.
21. Holmes, *Shaping of Peace*, p. 69.
22. Pearson, *Words and Occasions*, p. 71. Pearson, *Mike*, vol. 2, p. 244.
23. Pickersgill and Forster, *Mackenzie*, pp. 404-405.
24. Pearson, *Mike*, vol. 2, p. 111.
25. St. Laurent, in House of Commons, *Debates*, 1948, vol. 4, p. 3442.
26. Quoted in Escott Reid, *Envoy to Nehru* (Toronto: Oxford University Press, 1981), p. 21.
27. DEA, *Annual Report, 1949*, p. 18.
28. Robert Spencer, *Canada in World Affairs, 1946-49* (Toronto: Oxford University Press, 1959), pp. 270-71.

CHAPTER 3

1. Reid, *Time of Fear and Hope*, and James Eayrs, *In Defence of Canada* (Toronto: UTP, 1980), vol. 4, chapter 2.
2. L.B. Pearson, *Mike*, vol. 2.
3. House of Commons, *Debates*, vol. 6, 4 July 1947, p. 5078.
     DEA, (S/S) 47/12, 13 August 1947. Ibid., "Canada at the UN," 1947, pp. 178-80.
4. H.F. Armstrong, *New York Times Magazine*, 14 September 1947. Armstrong was the editor of *Foreign Affairs*, to which Pearson had already contributed an article.
5. Reid, *Time of Fear and Hope*, pp. 34-35.
6. Escott Reid, "The Birth of the North Atlantic Alliance," *International Journal* (Summer 1967), p. 247.
7. Pearson, *Mike*, vol. 2, pp. 150-60.
8. *Foreign Relations of the United States (FRUS)*, vol. 3, (Washington: Department of State, 1948), pp. 1-2.
9. Bullock, *Ernest Bevin*, p. 486. *FRUS*, p. 5.
10. Pearson, *Mike*, vol. 2, p. 43.
11. National Liberal Federation, Press Release, 20 January 1948. Pickersgill and Forster, *Mackenzie*, vol. 4, chapter 4.
12. DEA, file 283(s) contains an almost complete collection of documents relating to the negotiation of the treaty.
13. Wrong to DEA, 23 March, 1948, file 283(s).
14. Nicholas Henderson, *The Birth of Nato* (Boulder, Col.: Westview Press, 1983), p. 14. *FRUS*, Marshall to Bidault, p. 55.
15. Quoted in Reid, *Time of Fear and Hope*, pp. 135-36.
16. House of Commons, *Debates*, vol. 3, p. 2303.

17. NAC, Cabinet Conclusions, vol. RG 2A5A, reel T2366.

18. DEA, file 283(s), Reid to Pearson, 3 March 1948.

19. Ibid., Pearson to King, 27 March; and FRUS, 1948, vol. 3, pp. 59-72. The text of the so-called Pentagon Paper is printed in FRUS, 1948, vol. 3, pp. 72-75. For Canadian doubts see Pearson-Wrong exchange, DEA, file 283(s), 1 and 2 April.

20. Ibid., Pearson to King, 12 April 1948.

21. Ibid., Wrong to Pearson, 8 May, 7 April 1948.

22. Reid, *Time of Fear and Hope*, pp. 89-90, and James Reston, *New York Times*, 13 April 1948. Partial text in Pearson, *Mike*, vol 2, p. 52.

23. FRUS, 1948, vol. 3, p. 138.

24. On 29 April St. Laurent told the House of Commons: "Pending the strengthening of the UN, we should be willing to associate ourselves with other free states in any appropriate collective security arrangement which may be worked out under Articles 51 and 52 of the Charter." House of Commons, *Debates*, 1948, vol. 4, pp. 3448-50.

25. DEA, file 283(s), Wrong to Reid, 17 June 1948.

26. Ibid., Reid to Pearson, 26 June 1948.

27. Ibid., Reid to file, 23 June 1948.

28. FRUS, 1948, vol.3, pp. 148-82.

29. Ibid., p. 157.

30. The only published account of these and the subsequent talks by a participant (aside from the brief references in *Mike*) is by Henderson in *The Birth of Nato*.

31. FRUS, 1948, vol. 3, pp. 175-76. DEA, file 283(s), Pearson to Vanier, 13 August. French views are described in ibid., Ritchie to Pearson, 23 August, reporting on a British demarche in Paris that day. Pearson memorandum, 20 August in ibid.

32. Text in FRUS, 1948, vol. 3, pp. 237ff.

33. Pearson, *Mike*, vol. 2, p. 55.

34. FRUS, 1948, vol. 3, p. 239.

35. Pearson, *Mike*, vol. 2, p. 55.

36. DEA, file 283(s), Memorandum to Cabinet, 4 October 1948. NAC, RG2 A5A, reel T2366, Cabinet Conclusions.

37. Text in DEA, "External Affairs," November 1948.

38. This document, entitled "Commentary on the Washington paper of September 9, 1948," 6 December 1948, is printed in Eayrs, *In Defence of Canada*, DEA file 283(s), pp. 371-73.

39. DEA, file 283(s), Pearson to Wrong, 4 January 1949, and Wrong to Reid, 8 January 1949.

40. Ibid., Pearson to Wrong, 18 January 1949.

41. Pearson, *Mike*, vol. 2. p. 60. Wrong was the older friend and was closer to Acheson in temperament.

42. DEA, file 283(s), Reid to Wrong, 7 February. Wrong to DEA, 9 February 1949 and FRUS, 1949, vol. 4, pp. 85-86.

43. DEA, file 283(s), Pearson to Wrong, and Wrong to Pearson, 17 and 19 February 1949.

44. House of Commons, *Debates*, 28 March 1949, vol. 3, p. 2098.

45. NAC, RG2 A5A, reel T2367, Cabinet Conclusions.
46. DEA, S/S, 49/12, p. 7.
47. Pearson, *Mike*, vol. 2, p. 64.
48. Lester Pearson, "Canada and the North Atlantic Alliance," *Foreign Affairs* (April 1949), pp. 374-75.
49. Bullock, *Bevin*, p. 672.

CHAPTER 4

1.   DEA, S/S 49/14, p. 1.
2.   DEA, file 50017-40/2, Memo to Cabinet, 17 March 1950; ibid., St. Laurent to Nehru, 31 March 1949.
3.   Most of the diary notes he kept at the time are printed in *Mike*, vol. 2, pp. 108-16. The text of the declaration is in DEA, *Annual Report, 1949*, p. 18.
4.   NAC, Pearson Papers, MG26 N1, vol. 23, "Notes on visit to London."
5.   Ibid., Prime Ministers' Meetings (PMM), (49), 6th meeting, p. 4. House of Commons, *Debates*, 1949, vol. 3, p. 1103.
6.   DEA, "External Affairs," March 1950, p. 79.
7.   Ibid., p. 82.
8.   The best Canadian account of the meeting is in Douglas LePan, *Bright Glass of Memory* (Scarborough, Ont.: McGraw-Hill Ryerson, 1979), pp. 145-80. Escott Reid has also published his impressions of Colombo in *Radical Mandarin*, pp. 245-52. LePan and Reid were the senior economic and political advisers respectively to Pearson at Colombo. A partial text of this statement is in DEA, "External Affairs," p. 87.
9.   Pearson, *Mike*, vol. 2, p. 119.
10. Bullock, *Bevin*, p. 745.
11. Lepan, *Bright Glass*, p. 233.
12. DEA, "External Affairs," p. 81. NAC, Pearson Papers, MG22 N1, vol. 22, "Survey of Strategic Situation," January 1950.
13   DEA, "External Affairs," p. 90. Pearson, *Mike*, vol. 2, pp. 128-29.
14. Ibid., p. 128.
15. LePan, *Bright Glass*, p. 187. LePan's account of the Sydney conference is authoritative on the Canadian approach to the issue.
16. Pearson, *Mike*, vol. 2, pp. 120-21.
17. NAC, RG2 A5A, reel T2368, Cabinet Conclusions, 12 June 1950.
18. House of Commons, *Debates*, 1950, vol. 4, pp. 4370-74.
19. NAC, RG258687/160, box 131, file 11038-40, "draft instructions," 1 September 1950.
20. Ibid., Ottawa to London, 16 September 1950.
21. Ibid., Memorandum to Cabinet, 24 October 1950.
22. LePan, *Bright Glass*, p. 213.
23. NAC, Memorandum to Cabinet, 24 October 1950.
24. Cabinet Conclusions, meetings of 25 October, 1 and 8 November 1950.

25. LePan, *Bright Glass*, p. 128.
26. NAC, RG258687/160, box 131, file 11038-40, "Press Reaction to the Colombo Plan," 21 December 1950.
27. NAC, RG258687/160, box 131, file 11038-40, 27 December 1950.
28. Cabinet Conclusions, meeting of 28 December 1950.
29. LePan, *Bright Glass*, p. 218. NAC, RG258687, Pearson to Abbott, 17 January 1951.
30. DEA, S/S 51/4, 2 February 1951.
31. NAC, file 11038-40, Cabinet Decisions, 7 February 1951.
32. House of Commons, *Debates*, vol. 1, 1951, p. 537.
33. Escott Reid, *Envoy to Nehru* (Toronto: Oxford University Press, 1981, p. 18,) LePan, *Bright Glass*, p. 222.
34. Wynne Plumptre, "Perspectives on Our Aid to Others," *International Journal* (Summer 1967).
35. L.B. Pearson, "The Development of Canadian Foreign Policy," *Foreign Affairs* (October 1951), pp. 20-21.

CHAPTER 5

1. DEA, "External Affairs," (March 1950), p. 79. *Mike*, vol. 2, pp. 163-64.
2. Acheson, *Present at the Creation*, p. 357, pp. 379-80.
3. NAC, Pearson Papers, MG26 N1, vol. 65, "Pearson to St. Laurent," 14 April 1950. *FRUS*, 1950, vol. 1, pp. 276, 282. This study, subsequently known as NSC-68, was not approved by the president until September, after the Korean War provided him with the excuse to begin implementing its alarming implications for the US budget.
4. DEA, "External Affairs" (April 1950).
5. Acheson, *Present at the Creation*, p. 377.
6. *FRUS*, 1950, vol. 1, p. 287. *FRUS*, 1950, vol. 7 (Korea), pp. 149, 158, 199.
7. Harry Truman, *Years of Trial and Hope* (New York: Signet Books, 1965), p. 378.
8. House of Commons, *Debates*, 26 June 1950, pp. 4116-17.
9. Text in DEA, *Canada and the Koran Crisis* (Ottawa: King's Printer, 1950), p. 21.
10. NAC, RG2, Series 16, vol. 20, Cabinet Conclusions, 27 and 28 June 1950.
11. Ibid., 29 June 1950. A summary of Quebec editorial comment is in Denis Stairs, *The Diplomacy of Constraint* (Toronto: UTP, 1974), p. 58. House of Commons, *Debates*, 30 June 1950, p. 4459.
12. *Canada and the Korean Crisis*, p. 27.
13. NAC, RG2, Series 16, vol. 20, Cabinet Conclusions, 12 July 1950.
14. DEA, S/S 50/26, 14 July 1950.
15. *FRUS*, 1950, vol. 7, pp. 329, 372.
16 DEA, file 50069-A-40, Pearson to Wrong, 13 July 1950.
17. *FRUS*, 1950, vol. 7, p. 397.
18. Ibid., Acheson to Nehru, 25 July 1950, p. 466.
19. Cabinet Conclusions, 19 July 1950. *Mike*, vol 2, p. 165. See also Paul Martin, *A*

Very Public Life, vol. 2, p. 94

20. Bothwell and Kilbourn, *C.D. Howe* (Toronto: McClleland and Stewart, 1979), p. 252.

21. *FRUS*, 1950, vol. 7, pp. 462-64, p. 489.

22. NAC, Pearson Papers, memorandum to St. Laurent, 1 August 1950.

23. *FRUS*, 1950, vol. 7, p. 502. This was not George Kennan's view. He believed that "the Soviet communists did not launch the Korean operation as a first step in a world war...they simply wanted control of South Korea" and took advantage of "favourable circumstances." *FRUS*, 1950, vol. 1, p. 361.

24. Cabinet Conclusions, vol. 21, 2, 3, 15, and 18 August. *Canada and the Korean Crisis*, pp. 31-35, radio address by the Prime Minister.

25. DEA, file 50069-A-40, Washington telegram 1701, 5 August 1950.

26. Pearson Papers, Pearson to Acheson, 15 August 1950, Pearson to Hickerson, 10 August 1950.

27. Ibid., Acheson to Pearson, 9 September 1950.

28. House of Commons, *Debates*, 31 August 1950, pp. 94, 96.

29. Pearson Papers, DEA memo, 8 December 1950, "Canada and Korea."

30. *FRUS*, 1950, vol. 7, p. 773. The British were the only American ally to have provided troops on the ground at this stage, and it suited both governments that the British take the lead in marshalling political support for US objectives in Korea - the British in order to influence these objectives, and the Americans in order to give them legitimacy through the UN.

31. *Documents on the Korean Crisis*, p. 4.

32. There is a wealth of documentation on Indian views as seen through the eyes of the diligent US Ambassador in New Delhi, Loy Henderson, in *FRUS*, 1950, vol. 7. In contrast, nothing is reported from Ottawa. The government of India was the main channel to Peking, depending in turn on the reports of Ambassador Pannikar, who has described his role as messenger (and more) in *Two Chinas* (London: Allen and Unwin, 1955), pp. 102-24.

33. Cabinet Conclusions, 4 October 1950.

34. *FRUS*, 1950, vol. 7, pp. 885, 893. Pearson Papers, DEA memo, 8 December 1950. This summary of events in October and November differs from the account in Pearson's memoirs. The latter suggests that Acheson agreed to a delay in military operations for "three to four days," but this claim is not supported by the summary. Pearson, *Mike*, vol. 2, pp. 178-79.

35. Acheson, *Present at the Creation*, p. 466.

36. Reid, *Radical Mandarin*, p. 260.

37. DEA, S/S 51/4, "Review of the International Situation," 2 February 1951. Peter Gellman has explored the contrast between the rhetoric of collective security and Pearson's practice in this case, without, however, giving due weight to the fact that Pearson had to balance his instinctive preference for caution against the strong opinions of Canada's principal allies, who were doing the actual fighting. See Gellman, "Lester B. Pearson, Collective Security, and the World Order Tradition of Canadian Foreign Policy," *International Journal* (Winter 1988-89).

38. Pearson Papers, DEA memo, "Assurances from General MacArthur," 9 December 1950.
39. Ibid., 8 December 1950.
40. Pearson Papers, transcript of press conference held 30 November 1950.
41. Ibid., DEA memo, "Summary of reactions in foreign offices abroad to our memo of 2 December on Korea," 9 December 1950. *Documents on the Korean Crisis*, p. 16, Cabinet Conclusions, 6 December 1950.
42. Pearson Papers, DEA memo, "The International crisis arising out of the defeat of UN forces in Korea," 9 December 1950.
43. Cabinet Conclusions, 13, 21, 28 December 1950.
44. See *Mike*, vol. 2, appendix one, for a detailed account of the activities of the Ceasefire Committee, based on Pearson's diary. This was one of the few occasions after 1948 when he kept a diary record of events. The account in Stairs, *The Diplomacy of Constraint*, chapter 5, is the best critical examination of Canadian policies during this period.
45. They were to be badly strained in the autumn of 1952, however, when Acheson believed that Pearson was dealing with the Indian government behind his back. Pearson was president of the General Assembly at the time and was acting in this capacity on Korean matters. See *Mike*, vol. 2, p. 207.
46. DEA, S/S 51/14, 10 April 1951.
47. Prime Minister Attlee had rushed to Washington in early December 1950, to find out if Truman was considering atomic retaliation on China. He was not, and Attlee so informed the Canadian cabinet on 9 December. One of his advisers told the department, however, that "the UK would have to support the US in whatever course the latter decided to take." See Pearson Papers, memo of 12 December 1950.
48. They did so under the "Uniting for Peace" resolution adopted on 3 November 1950 with only the Soviet bloc voting against.
49. DEA, *Documents on the Korean Crisis*, pp. 8-9.

CHAPTER 6

1. DEA, *Documents on the Korean Crisis*, p. 17.
2. DEA, file 50069-C-40, "Views of the Canadian Government on Possible Use of Atomic Weapons in the Far East," 6 December 1950.
3. Ibid., "Memo of Conversation Between R.G. Arneson, Special Assistant to the Secretary of State on Atomic Energy, and G. Ignatieff," 6 December 1950.
4. NAC, RG2 A5A, reel T2368, Cabinet Conclusions, 9 December 1950. Dean Rusk, who was then a senior State Department official, has confirmed that the option of using nuclear weapons was never seriously considered "since Truman refused to go down that trail." See Rusk, *As I Saw It*, p. 170.
5. Pearson, *Mike*, vol. 1, p. 264.
6. See, for example, McGeorge Bundy, *Danger and Survival* (New York: Random House, 1988), chapter 4.

7.   House of Commons, *Debates*, vol. 1, p. 429.

8.   Roger Dingman, "Atomic Diplomacy during the Korean War," International Security (Winter 1988/89), p. 59. A best-guess estimate of the size of the US stockpile of atomic weapons at this time is about three hundred. See also Bundy, *Danger and Survival*, p. 203.

9.   USAF to Chief of Air Staff, Ottawa, 18 August 1950, and DEA memo, file 50195-40, 6 October 1950. This file contains an incomplete account of this curious episode, mainly because neither the embassy in Washington nor External Affairs were informed of the USAF request in August. The embassy was given an American version of the facts on 1 December when the State Department asked about how to obtain permission for the next transfer of "special weapons" to Goose Bay "probably next spring" (ibid., Embassy Washington letter 3088, 2 December 1950). Cabinet Conclusions, 25 October 1950.

10. DEA, file 50069-C-40, Ambassador, Washington, to USSEA, 3201, 9 December 1950.

11. Ibid., Ambassador, Washington, to USSEA, 19, 3 January 3 1951.

12. DEA memo, Pearson to Heeney, 9 February, 20 March 1951. This and other papers on this file have been extensively cited by James Eayrs in vol. 4 of his series *In Defence of Canada*. Eayrs treats separately the two main issues involved; storage of nuclear weapons at Goose Bay, and the demand for consultation on atomic strategy, although they were closely linked. He breaks off his account in early May 1951.

13. DEA, file 50069-C-40, USSEA to Ambassador, Washington, 4 May 1951.

14. Ibid., Notes of meeting on 17 May attended by Pearson, Wrong, Heeney, and Norman Robertson, 22 May 1951.

15. *FRUS*, 1951, vol. 1, pp. 841-42.

16. Pearson Papers, vol. 17, Pearson to Wrong, 24 May 1951. NAC, file RG2 A5A, reel T2369, Cabinet Conclusions, 8 May 1951.

17. *FRUS*, 1951, vol. 1, pp. 843-44.

18. Ibid., pp. 845-53. I was unable to locate the Canadian records for this and the two subsequent meetings in 1951, nor for the three meetings in 1952. The US records for the meetings in 1951 are in *FRUS* and the meetings in 1952 are noted but not recorded in *FRUS*, 1952, vol. 6.

19. Ibid., pp. 855-56 and 859-64.

20. Ibid., pp. 894-96, Deputy of Secretary of Defence Lovett to Acheson, 5 November 1951. The British obtained a similar "consent" agreement in October 1951.

21. Ibid., part 2, p. 2032. See also Bundy, *Danger and Survival*, p. 231: "Truman never came close to the use of nuclear weapons in Korea."

22. Pearson Papers, vol. 45, DEA memo, 5 September 1952, "Visit of SSEA to Washington."

23. *Documents on Canadian External Relations* (DCER) vol. 18, 1952, Minister of Supply and Services, 1990, p. 719. Churchill told the cabinet on a visit to Ottawa in January 1952 that the first test of a British atomic weapon that

summer "might have substantial influence on US readiness to exchange information on atomic development." Ibid., p. 1085.

24. Pearson, *Mike*, vol. 2, p. 208.

25. Pearson Papers, "Memo to the P.M.," 18 February 1953. Cabinet Conclusions, 21 January. *DCER*, 1953, Joint Communiqué on occasion of visit of Prime Minister to Washington, 8 May 1953, pp. 1003ff.

26. DEA, file 50209-40, Ambassador, Washington, to SSEA, 23 October 1953.

27. Ibid., SSEA to Ambassador, Washington, 5 November 1953. House of Commons, *Debates*, Appendix to proceedings of 14 November 1953, pp. 24-28. Quoted in R.F. Swanson, *Canadian-American Summit Diplomacy 1923-1973*, (Ottawa: Carleton Library, 1975), p. 157.

28. Quoted in Bundy, *Danger and Survival*, p. 246.

29. Pearson Papers, vol. 65, "Memo to Prime Minister," 2 February 1954.

30. Quoted in Eayrs, *In Defence of Canada*, vol. 4, p. 253.

31. "A Look at the New Look," S/S 54/16, 15 March 1954.

32. Pearson Papers, "Memo of a Conversation with John Foster Dulles," 18 March 1954.

33. House of Commons, *Debates*, 1953-54, vol. 4, pp. 3328-31.

34. *FRUS*, 1954, vol. 1, part 1, pp. 1, pp. 1198-99 and 1237. Bundy, who was later to serve in the White House himself and was familiar with high-level decision-making, absolves Eisenhower of any serious intention to use nuclear weapons in support of the French, but is less charitable about the conduct of Dulles. Bundy, *Danger and Survival*, pp. 260-70.

35. DEA, file 50052-40, vol. 19, London to USSEA, 9 April 1954. Douglas Ross, *In the Interests of Peace: Canada and Vietnam* (Toronto: UTP, 1984), p. 45. Smith remembers the event but not the details. The absence of any written record suggests that he did not hear the conversation. Pearson told the Standing Committee on External Affairs on 6 April that the only way Canada could be involved in the war would be in response to a UN decision (Minutes of Proceedings and Evidence, 6 April, p. 25).

36. DEA, file 50219-40, Embassy, Washington to USSEA, 9 March 1954.

37. Ibid., 27 September 1954. DEA, file 50209-40, Memo for the Prime Minister, 8 December 1954.

38. Pearson, *Mike*, vol 2, p. 90. House of Commons, *Debates*, 20 January 1955, vol. 1, p. 362.

39. Pearson Papers, vol. 65, Memo for the Prime Minister, 17 March 1955.

40. DEA, file 50219-AE-40, Note of meeting between Pearson and Defence Minister Campney, 18 February 1955.

41. Ibid., file 50056-B-40, vol. 5, Memo of 14 March 1955.

42. *FRUS*, 1955-57, vol. 2, pp. 346-59. Pearson Papers, Memo for Prime Minister, 17 March 1955.

43. "Non-Military Co-operation in NATO," NATO Letter Special Supplement, 1 January 1957, p. 7.

44. S/S 55/5, 6 March 1955.

45. Pearson Papers, vol. 32, USSEA to Embassy Brussels, 4 April 1955. Lester B.

Pearson, *Democracy in World Politics* (Toronto: Saunders, 1955), pp. 18-25. The lectures were drafted by Arnold Smith, and extensively revised by Pearson. Reviews of the book were mostly favourable. Walter Lippman, probably the most influential American columnist of the day, wrote to Pearson: "I do not need to tell you how deeply in sympathy I am with the whole point of view and doctrine" (NAC, Smith Papers, MG31 E47, vol. 82, file 6)

46.   Pearson, *Mike*, vol 2, p. 228.

47.   By the end of the decade, as leader of the opposition, he was still wondering whether tactical nuclear weapons could be fired without bringing "death to civilians far from any battlefield." If they did, he implied, they should not be used by Canadian forces. See Pearson Papers, vol. 13, letter to Victor Sifton, 30 December 1959.

CHAPTER 7

1.   House of Commons, *Debates*, 1950, vol. 1, p. 132.
2.   The issue is discussed at length in Eayrs, *In Defence of Canada*, vol. 5, pp. 13-26.
3.   Ibid., p. 28 and RG2, vol. 2651, Cabinet Conclusions, 21 August 1952.
4.   *FRUS*, 1952-54, vol. 6, p. 2068.
5.   House of Commons, *Debates*, 1952-53, vol. 6, p. 2068.
6.   NAC, Pearson Papers, MG2 6N, vol. 36, record of talks with Department of State, 7 May 1953
7.   S/S 53/29, "Far Eastern Issues," 27 May 1953.
8.   *FRUS*, 1954, vol. 12, part 1, pp. 949-53, 1007.
9.   Ibid., p. 971, "US Objectives and courses of Action with Respect to South East Asia," 16 January 1954.
10. Pearson Papers, Memo of conversation with Dulles, 16 March 1954.
11. DEA, file 50052, Memo to Minister, 27 February 1954.
12. House of Commons, *Debates*, 1953-54, vol. 4, p. 3327. DEA, file 50052-40, USSEA to CBC International Service, 2 April 1954.
13. Department of State Bulletin, 12 April 1954.
14. House of Commons, *Debates*, 1953-54, vol. 3, pp. 3542-43.
15. DEA, file 50052-40, Heeney to Pearson, 7 April 1954; *FRUS*, 1952-54, p. 1275-78.
16. DEA, file 50052-40, High Commissioner, London to USSEA, 9 April 1954.
17. Cabinet Conclusions, 14 April 1954. Ibid., Transcript of interview with Robert Reford, 23 April 1954.
18. Ibid., Canadian Delegation, Geneva to USSEA, 27 and 28 April 1954.
19. *FRUS*, vol. 13, 27 and 29 April 1954, pp. 1168, 1423 and 1434-45.
20. S/S 54/28, 4 May 1954.
21. Pearson Papers, vol. 34, Pearson to St. Laurent, 6 May.
22. John Holmes, "Geneva 1954," *International Journal* (Summer 1967). Holmes was a close adviser to Pearson at Geneva and his account of the conference and of Pearson's activities there is authoritative.

23. *FRUS*, 1954, vol. 13, pp. 1523, 1549

24. NAC, RG2 vol. 2655, Cabinet Conclusions, 25 May 1954.

25. House of Commons, *Debates*, 1953-54, vol. 5, pp. 5188-92.

26. Ibid., pp. 5194-98.

27. S/S 54/31, 4 June 1954

28. DEA, file 50052-40, High Commissioner New Delhi to SSEA, 6 May 1954.

29. Ibid., Canadian Delegation, Geneva to USSEA, 28 May, 1 and 10 June 1954.

30. The speech is summarized in Embassy Paris despatch 974 of 17 June, of which I was in fact the author, having been posted to Paris eight months earlier and assigned the job of reporting on the French domestic scene. Mendès-France was a breath of fresh air to observers like myself because he left no doubt of where he stood on the issues and had great dramatic flair. In one instance, he brought to the podium of the National Assembly a glass of milk in a heroic but futile attempt to persuade his countrymen to drink less wine.

31. *FRUS*, 1954, vol. 13, p. 1717. DEA, file 50052-40, Canadian Delegation, Geneva to USSEA, 16 June 1954.

32. Ibid., 18-19, 22, 24, 26 June 1954.

33. *FRUS*, 1954, vol. 13, pp. 1830-31. DEA, file 50052-40, Washington Embassy to USSEA, 17 July 1954.

34. Texts of the Vietnam Cease-fire Agreement and the Final Declaration are reprinted in Douglas Ross, *In the Interests of Peace: Canada and Vietnam* (Toronto: UTP, 1984). Ross gives an excellent summary of the events surrounding the Geneva conference and Canadian attitudes thereto, although he makes little use of official material.

35. *Ottawa Journal*, 19 July 1954. DEA, file 50052-40, Geneva to USSEA, 19, 20, July 1954.

36. RG2, vol. 2655, Cabinet Conclusions, 22, 28 July 1954.

37. Pearson Papers, vol. 34, "Note on Discussion at Canadian Embassy, Washington," 28 June 1954.

38. Cabinet Conclusions, 22 July 1954.

39. DEA, file 50052-40, Embassy Washington, to USSEA, 24 July 1954. Privately, Dulles commented that Canada "could at least vote against Poland and India." See *FRUS*, p. 1857.

40. DEA, file 50052-40, Mackay to MacDonnel, 28 July 1954.

41. Ibid., Press Release, 29 July 1954.

42. Pearson Papers, vol. 34, Notes to Under-Secretary, 10 November 1954 and 18 February 1955.

CHAPTER 8

1. L.B. Pearson, "The Development of Canadian Foreign Policy," *Foreign Affairs*, (October 1951), pp. 20-24.

2. See, for example, speeches at Harvard University, 11 June 1953 (S/S 53/30), and at Dartmouth College, 14 June 1953 (S/S 53/31).

3. This was the title of the article in *World* magazine in December 1953, reprinted in S/S 53/50

4. NAC, RG2, reels T2367 and 2368, Cabinet Conclusions, 16 November, 21 December 1949, 7 March, 14 June, and 21 June 1950.

5. NAC, Wrong Papers, MG3 E101, Memo of conversation, 16 February 1950. DEA, file 50055-B-40, Pearson to St. Laurent, 24 January 1950. Cabinet Conclusions, 7 March 1950.

6. Ibid., 4 May, 14, 21 June 1950.

7. DEA, file 50055-B-40, Cabinet minute on instructions for Canadian delegation to UN General Assembly, 12 September 1950.

8. Pearson Papers, vol. 35, Wrong to Pearson, 16 February 1950.

9. *DCER*, vol. 18, Memo to Cabinet, 6 October 1952, pp. 166-67.

10. Peter Stursberg, *Lester Pearson and the American Dilemma* (Toronto: Doubleday, 1980), p. 122. Chester Ronning was present at the meeting with Chou, whom Ronning knew from his time in China, and is the source of the Stursberg account.

11. S/S 54/49, 7 November 1954.

12. Pearson Papers, vol. 4, "Memo of Conversation," 18 February 1953.

13. Ibid., vol. 65, 18 March 1954. J.L. Gaddis, *The Long Peace* (London: Oxford University Press, 1987), pp. 180-82, gives an excellent summary of American plans to exert "pressure" on China, and of the domestic pressures tending to freeze administration policy.

14. Text in "Report of the Committee on Foreign Relations, US Senate," 8 February 1955. For background see H.W. Brands Jr., "Testing Massive Retaliation," and Gordon Chang, "To the Nuclear Brink," *International Security* (Spring 1988).

15. Public papers of the President, 1955 (Washington: US Government Printing Office, 1959), p. 207.

16. Pearson Papers, vol. 65, Memo to Under-secretary, 7 January 1955.

17. S/S 55/2, 25 February 1955.

18. DEA, file 50056-B-40, Embassy Washington to SSEA, 28 January 1955.

19. S/S 55/4, 28 January 1955.

20. Pearson Papers, vol. 19, diary for 2 February 1955, p. 10.

21. *FRUS*, 1955-57, vol. 2, "Churchill to Eisenhower," n.d., p. 270.

22. Pearson Papers, vol. 19, diary for 5 February, p. 15.

23. DEA, file 50056-B-40, Embassy Washington to DEA, 7 February 1955; Pearson Papers, vol. 19, and diary.

24. RG2, vol. 2657, Cabinet Conclusions, 14 February 1955.

25. DEA, file 50056-B-40, Pearson to USSEA, 16 February, Pearson to Robertson, 17 February, and Pearson to Reid, 19 February.

26. *FRUS*, 1955-57, vol. 2, pp. 280-86.

27. DEA, file 50056-B-40, New Delhi to DEA, 22, 26 February 1955, Pearson to Embassy Washington, 7 March 1955.

28. *FRUS*, 1955-57, vol. 2, pp. 261, 346-47, 377.

29. *New York Times*, 29 March 1955.

30. Cabinet Conclusions, 18 March 1955, text in Pearson Papers, vol. 32.

31. Ibid., Memo to Prime Minister, 19 March 1955.
32. S/S 55/10, 24 March 1955. S/S 55/14, 21 April 1955.
33. Pearson Papers, vol. 32, Memo to Minister, 4 and 5 April 1955. RG2, vol. 2657, Cabinet Conclusions, 29 April 1955.
34. *FRUS*, 1955-57, vol. 2, pp. 475-76, 494-95, and 519-20.
35. J.B. Martin, *Adlai Stevenson and the World* (New York: Doubleday, 1977), pp. 173-75.
36. S/S 55/30, 25 August 1955. Pearson Papers, vol. 20, Memo to USSEA, 12 September 1955. S/S 56/2, 31 January 1956.
37. The phrase is Holmes's, in *The Shaping of Peace*, vol. 2, p. 200.
38. Ibid., p. 184. Holmes was present at the conference of Commonwealth prime ministers in June 1956 when St. Laurent expressed this fear.

CHAPTER 9

1. Pearson, *Mike*, vol. 2, p. 240.
2. Ibid., p. 245.
3. Ibid., pp. 248-51.
4. NAC, RG2, vol. 2658, Cabinet Conclusions, 16 September 1955.
5. House of Commons, *Debates*, 1956, vol. 1, p. 777.
6. Holmes, *The Shaping of Peace*, p. 353.
7. NAC, Pearson Papers, vol. 8, letter to T.W.L. Macdermot, 3 March 1956.
8. RG2, vol. 5775, Cabinet Conclusions, 15 March 1956.
9. Pearson, *Mike*, vol. 2, pp. 252-54.
10. Cabinet Conclusions, 10 May, 27, 31, July 1956.
11. *FRUS*, 1955-57, vol. 16, pp. 31, 74.
12. Ibid., p. 10.
13. Pearson, *Mike*, vol. 2, p. 256.
14. *FRUS*, 1955-57, Eisenhower to Eden, 31 July 1956, pp. 69-70.
15. DEA, file 50372-40, Chairman, Chiefs of Staff to USSEA, 3 August 1956.
16. Cabinet Conclusions, 29 August 1956.
17. Pearson Papers, vol. 37, Pearson to Prime Minister, 3 September 1956.
18. The fullest accounts of the conspiracy and the reasons motivating the three belligerents are in Terence Robertson, *Crisis: The Inside Story of the Suez Conspiracy* (Toronto: McClelland and Stewart, 1964). Pearson gave Robertson access to his papers, somewhat to the discomfort of External Affairs. See also Roger Louis and Roger Owen, *Suez, 1956 - The Crisis and its Consequences* (London: Oxford University Press, 1989); and Keith Kyle, *Suez* (New York: St. Martin's Press, 1991).
19. Cabinet Conclusions, 27 September 1956.
20. DEA, file 50372-40, Embassy Paris to USSEA, 24 September 1956. Cabinet Conclusions, 20 September 1956. High Commissioner, London to DEA, 17 October, and Permanent Mission, NY to DEA, 26 October
21. Ibid., Embassy Paris to DEA, 3 and 17 October. Gladwyn Jebb, British

ambassador to France, has commented: "Something was happening completely outside the diplomatic machine of which I had no inkling" (*Memoirs* [London: Weidenfeld and Nicholson, 1972], p. 282). Robert Rhodes James, *Anthony Eden*, (London: Papermac, 1987), pp. 528-31.

22. DEA, file 50372-40, Embassy Washington to DEA, 19 October 1956.

23. *FRUS*, 1955-57, vol. 16, pp. 640-42.

24. From my post at the embassy in Paris I wrote to my father on 1 November, after Franco-British intervention had begun: "In all of this the Americans have not been very intelligent. They have not understood the profound malaise in this country, its back-to-the-wall, dog in the manger frame of mind. You remember the days before the fall of Dien Bien Phu [in 1954]. It is the same now. A sort of blind hitting out at the 20th century and all the calamities it has brought to France." A week later I learned from a colleague at the Israeli embassy, and so reported home, that the timing of the Israeli attack was related to Soviet intervention in Hungary on 24 October. He said they had originally planned to wait until after the American presidential elections on 3 November.

25. For American knowledge of these manoeuvres, see *FRUS*, 1955-57, vol. 16, pp. 802 and 815-50.

26. DEA, *Crisis in the Middle East* (Ottawa: Queen's Printer, 1957), p. 6.

27. Pearson Papers, Eden to St. Laurent, 20 October 1956. Holmes, *The Shaping of Peace*, vol. 2, p. 356.

28. Pearson Papers, Pearson to Robertson and Pearson to Heeney, 30 October 1956.

29. Cabinet Conclusions, 31 October 1956

30. Text in Pearson, *Mike*, vol. 2, pp. 269-71.

31. Cabinet Conclusions, 1 November 1956. DEA, file 50134-40, Robertson to Pearson, 1 November 1956.

32. Ibid., DEA, file 50134-40, Permanent Mission to DEA, 2 November 1956

33. *Crisis in the Middle East*, p. 10, and Thomson, *Louis St. Laurent*, p. 472.

34. Pearson Papers, Holmes to Pearson, 6 December 1956.

35. *FRUS*, 1955-57, vol. 16, p. 941.

36. Pearson Papers, Heeney to file, 3 November 1956.

37. *FRUS*, 1955-57, vol. 16, pp. 941-42.

38. Cabinet Conclusions, 3 November 1956.

39. Pearson Papers, Heeney to file, 3 November 1956.

40. Pearson, *Mike*, vol. 2, p. 284. Pearson Papers, Heeney to file, 4 November 1956.

41. Ibid., Memo to Minister, 3 November 1956.

42. Pearson, *Mike*, vol. 2, p. 284. *FRUS*, 1955-57, vol. 16, pp. 479-80.

43. Pearson Papers, Holmes to Pearson, 6 December 1956.

44. DEA, file 50134-40, Permis New York to DEA, 4 November 1956.

45. Ibid., Pearson to DEA, 5 November 1956.

46. Text in Pearson, *Mike*, vol. 2, p. 289.

47. NAC, Reid Papers, MG31 E46, vol. 8, file 24, Escott Reid to DEA, 6 and 7 November 1956.

48. S/S 56/25, "The Situation in Hungary," 4 November 1956.

49. Cabinet Conclusions, 7 November 1956.

50.   Pearson, *Mike*, vol. 2, pp. 302-6. Memo to Prime Minister, 15 November 1956, and summary of telegrams relating to Canadian participation in UNEF, 5 December 1956.

51.   Presentation by G. Jahn, Chairman of Norwegian Nobel Committee, 10 December 1957, reprinted in *Nobel Lectures, Peace, 1951-1970, Vol. 3* (Oslo: Elsevier Publishing Company, 1972), p. 125.

52.   House of Commons, *Debates*, 4th (Special) Session, 26 November 1956, pp. 18, 53, 55.

53.   Ibid., p. 64.

CHAPTER 10

1.   DEA, S/S 57/27, 5 April 1957.

2.   *Maclean's* magazine, 6 July 1957.

3.   Draft material for memoirs, 14 November 1972. Text in possession of author.

4.   House of Commons, *Debates*, vol. 4, pp. 3448-49, 28 April 1948.

5.   Pearson still felt this way in 1957. See his Nobel Lecture, "The Four Faces of Peace"; reprinted in L. B. Pearson, *Diplomacy in the Nuclear Age* (Toronto: Saunders, 1959), p. 103.

6.   Address to Atlantic Award dinner, 11 June 1966; reprinted in *Words and Occasions*, p. 259.

7.   House of Commons, *Debates*, vol. 4, p. 3011, 14 May 1951.

8.   House of Commons, *Debates*, 7 August 1950; Pearson to General Assembly, 27 September 1950.

9.   Pearson to General Assembly, 3 November 1950.

10.   Pearson to *New York Herald Tribune Forum*, 29 October 1950.

11.   Pearson, "The Development of Canadian Foreign Policy," *Foreign Affairs* (October 1951), pp. 27-28.

12.   S/S 57/2, 14 January 1957. Pearson, "Force for UN," *Foreign Affairs* (April 1957), p. 401.

13.   "An Agenda for Peace," report of the Secretary General, UN, New York, 1992.

14.   *Maclean's* magazine, 6 July 1957.

15.   Denis Stairs, "Present in Moderation: Lester Pearson and the Craft of Diplomacy," *International Journal* (Winter 1973-74), p. 150.

16.   Pearson, *Mike*, vol. 2, p. 207.

17.   Hazel Erskine, "The Polls: Atomic Weapons and Nuclear Energy," *Public Opinion Quarterly* (Summer 1963), p. 181.

INDEX